FAITH IN FICTION DEVOTIONAL NO.1

WIZARDS, WARDROBES, & HALFLINGS

Wizards, Wardrobes, and Halflings

Faith in Fiction Devotional No.1,

Wizards, Wardrobes, & Halflings

Collected and Edited by
Christopher D. Schmitz

Entries by
Brett Armstrong
Christopher D. Schmitz
D. A. Randall
Kadee Karder

Table of Contents

Foreword

Like the other authors gathered here, I love speculative fiction. Distant galaxies, ancient civilizations, abandoned space stations, and odd creatures with funny names—these are the tropes of my literary adoration.

At the same time, we authors are all followers of Christ. Each of us has a personal story, an encounter with Christ's divinity that shaped not only our awareness of the world we live in, but directed our lives from then on.

Having written Christian speculative fiction for over a decade now, I can testify that these two adorations—one for the "What if?" and the other for the "He lives!"—often appear to be in conflict. This tension is no more clearly seen than in the perception of speculative fiction (specifically, science fiction, fantasy, and horror) written by Christians.

To the secular reader, such stories carry a level of (oftentimes deserved) skepticism. A wariness for being preached at, or having religiosity overwhelm the narrative, or a plot that feels too neat and tidy for today's complicated world. "We have computers now!" they scream. "You can't fix everything with a single prayer in a parking lot!"

Speculative fiction has an equally hard road in the Christian community. Anything that includes magic—aside from books written by Tolkien and Lewis—is seen as suspect. "Dragons? How could those possibly be used to show God's glory?" And don't get me started on vampires, zombies, and werewolves. Everyone knows monsters are evil. Aren't we supposed to think only on good things?

Plus, science fiction seems to presuppose a secular worldview. How is the Christmas star relevant when we can *visit* other stars? What does a Savior for humankind mean in a universe filled with other not-so-human-kind?

Speculative versus scripture, sacred versus the secular, *stories* versus *Truth*—there seems to be no easy way to rectify the two adorations. No way for the "What if?" and the "He lives!" to live together.

"Not so!" say I. They've been coexisting peacefully in my head and heart since childhood.

And within these pages you'll find others, like me, who cry "Not so!"

Here you'll find thoughtful and entertaining insights into daily living, fueled by the "What if?" Christian authors who've taken settings and characters from epic speculative worlds and applied them to the more mundane struggles of this Earthly sphere. A bridge between the adorations. The sacred and secular working together for a common good. Your good.

I'm delighted with what they've done. I pray you are too.

– Kerry Nietz
    Author of Amish Vampires in Space

Introduction

I grew up in the 1980s. It was a weird decade, and the ones that came after have proved confusing for nonChristians' view of believers (especially evangelicals.) In the 80s, anything featuring magic at all was villainized. Rock and Roll could literally send your children to hell, and churches spread the news that Dungeons and Dragons™ told teenagers to sacrifice cats and commit mass suicide while listening to Ozzy Osbourne albums. Strangely enough (by that I mean *sadly enough*), they spent more time freaking out and speculating over things that went bump in the night than they did sharing the Gospel of Christ.

Back in 1988 or 1989 I remember school shopping as a child. I wanted to get a folder that had a beautiful fantasy scene featuring a dragon on a rocky perch. My mother said no, because liking dragons was a gateway to Satanism.

Here we are, now, four decades later, and fantasy has hit mainstream, and even Christian bookstores despite it all. Harry Potter has become the best-selling book second only to the Holy Bible. There's not a child in America who isn't familiar with at least *one* of the major fantasy series on the market... and although American Christians might have discovered the truth (that the rampant terror of the 80s/90s were based on fear-mongering and half-truths), we've rarely realized the true joy of fantasy.

God has threaded creation with "general revelation," or the ability to see Him in and through many different aspects of creation: we see the splendor of it atop a mountain vista or in the hues of a sunset; we experience joy when welcoming a new life to the world; the glory of the universe reveals itself as we look through a microscope and realize how beautifully and wonderfully we are made, right down to the atomic level.

Fantasy delves that creativity endowed us by our eternally creative Designer. It is part of the Imago Dei (the Image of God.)

Often, we find symbols in our lives that are intimate representations of who we are. Mine became a dragon, not to spite my mother, but perhaps as a way of God foreshadowing events in my life that I would not have understood so long ago.

"Sleeping on a dragon's hoard with greedy, dragonish thoughts in his heart, he had become a dragon himself." C.S. Lewis, Voyage of the Dawn Treader, regarding Eustace Scrubb.

In life, we start as children and then become something more. Eustace had become a dragon, although quite on accident, in the Narnia series. It takes the power of Aslan (an allegory for Christ) to transform Eustace back into what God's purpose for him had been. That is my story, too, much as it also describes to others.

This is the power of fiction: that we connect *our* stories to *God's* stories and then live them out in front of our fellow man. In the process we create *new* stories, linking them to *each other* and then back again to our Creator. It is an amazing, interwoven thing.

–Christopher D. Schmitz ed.

About
Faith in Fiction
Devotionals

This book is a collaborative effort that grew out of an online community of faith-based speculative fiction writers (Realm Maker's Consortium on Facebook.) Each of the writers shares lessons from scripture and popular works of fiction that you might be familiar with, plus additional devotionals drawn out of a series that he or she writes. We wholeheartedly encourage you to read through this book and consider purchasing those stories written by the individual writers; we welcome any sharing or discussion you would like to engage in. Nothing pleases an author more than knowing that his or her readers are talking about/recommending their books to others.

Each set of devos pieces will have its own style and flair since they are written by different people; one thing they each have in common is a love of storytelling as a means to impart wisdom through Scripture. Each writer has a bio at the end of his or her set of devotional entries where their respective contact and follow information is listed.

About
The Chronicles of Narnia

The Chronicles of Narnia is a seven book series written by C. S. Lewis that was published in the 1950s. This series is Lewis's best known work and is considered a children's classic, though it is much beloved by adults, too, and has been adapted into almost every media format available at one time or another.

Featuring talking animals, magic, and mythic beasts, it is a fantasy series that features children from the real world entering a magic realm, making it one of the better known examples of "portal fiction." With a series released over several years and with a large chronology that draws off of internal events, the publication order and reading order are not the same, according to many fans of the series.

Of the well-known selections in this devotional book, The Chronicles of Narnia is easily the most recognizably faith based. Lewis wrote the series with several direct allegories in mind and has never obscured that fact or shied away from public discussion on the topic.

The Magician's Nephew

"Have this mind among yourselves, which is yours in Christ Jesus, Who, though He was in the form of God, did not count equality with God a thing to be grasped, but emptied Himself, by taking the form of a servant, being born in the likeness of men. And being found in human form, He humbled himself by becoming obedient to the point of death, even death on a cross."
Philippians 2:5-8 (ESV)

People love stories. I'm convinced that's why country music is so popular. From the perspective of this lay observer, country songs are tales of two varieties: wild happiness and crushing sorrow. That isn't too dissimilar to C. S. Lewis's *The Magician's Nephew*. First chronologically in *The Chronicles of Narnia* series, it has the joy of Narnia's creation and the tragedy of its corruption at the White Witch's arrival. Jadis, at one time, was merely a magically gifted noblewoman who wanted to rule her world, Charn. Her hunger for power made her into a monster. That's not figurative language, either; she destroyed her entire world because she couldn't accept any other ruler for that world.

Upon appearing in *The Magician's Nephew*, Jadis begins her quest for power afresh. She makes bold claims about conquering our world and deems people worthy of her time and interest based on how much magical potency she perceives they possess. Eventually she encounters Aslan for the first time. Here was real power, real majesty. Jadis watched him sing Narnia into existence and she hated Aslan. There are obvious reasons for it. He had more power than her and ruled a full, living world, whereas hers was dead and empty. Of course, she also sensed, to a degree, that Aslan was innately good and that she was not.

She schemes to become greater than Aslan, using magic fruit he created. Jadis must have convinced herself that he too was simply an ambitious being: someone who sought and found magic power. If she had truly understood Aslan then she wouldn't have attempted to resist him, to oppose him, and certainly not foolishly think she could destroy him. The parallels to how Man reacted in the early days after Creation are obvious. Man turned the joy of God's Garden to tragedy. Thinking we could become equals with God, we became the villains, rebels at war with God in His land. Like the White Witch, we cannot overcome Him. The end is our own destruction.

Another character in the book responsible for ruining Narnia's perfection, Diggory Kirke, didn't follow the White Witch into her folly. Not that she didn't tempt him. His backstory made her offer compelling. Diggory craved power too, his specifically being for the healing of his terminally ill mother. There is a moment in which all he need do is reach out and take that power and he could save his mother. Jadis urges him to join her. He was already an enemy to Aslan because he helped mar Narnia by bringing her there in the first place. Instead of deepening in his rebellion and joining Jadis's coup, Diggory decides to relent, to yield. He acknowledges his wrongs and makes amends with Aslan. He understood Aslan's right to rule and the restoration he experienced is a mirror to the renewal we enjoy when we rightly submit to God. When we truly understand who Christ is we don't resist His rule, we accept it, embrace it, and rejoice in it.

We live in a world that naturally gives rise to stories of tragedy and triumph. Crushing sorrow abounds, and Scripture tells us that it stems from us being all our similarity to Adam and Eve in our desire for self-rule. Jadis is a reflection of a tendency to exalt ourselves to our own harm and the harm of everyone and everything around us. But we aren't forced to make the same ill-fated choices. The entire expanse of Scripture gives a clear picture of the rightful ruler we may yield to and the inexpressible joy within that choice:

"Therefore God has highly exalted Him and bestowed on Him the name that is above every name, so that at the name of Jesus every knee should bow, in heaven and on earth and under the earth, and every tongue confess that Jesus Christ is Lord, to the glory of God the Father." --Philippians 2:9-11, ESV

The Lion, the Witch, and the Wardrobe

"...all three of them rolled over together in a happy laughing heap of fur and arms and legs. It was such a romp as no one had ever had except in Narnia; and whether it was more like playing with a thunderstorm or playing with a kitten Lucy could never make up her mind."

One of the most powerful lessons the Narnia series holds is the tenderness and approachability of God and His sovereign regality. It's especially potent in *The Lion, The Witch, and The Wardrobe*. The Great Lion, Aslan, is described in the most tender and affectionate of ways. To the point the reader longs to reach the out and stroke the fur of his mane and receive one of the "wild kisses" from his coarse tongue. At the same time, the first instance of the common refrain of the series that "he's not a tame lion" appears in the book. However soft the fur and forgiving he may be, we're never given the impression that we should take it for granted that he is affectionate towards anyone. When first describing Aslan to the children, the Beavers didn't offer any soft handed truisms.

"If there's anyone who can appear before Aslan without their knees knocking, they're either braver than most or else just silly."

"Then he isn't safe?" said Lucy.

"Safe?" said Mr. Beaver. "Don't you hear what Mrs. Beaver tells you? Who said anything about safe? 'Course he isn't safe. But he's good. He's the King, I tell you."

Later when they finally meet Aslan, their reaction to meeting him is hardly what you'd expect in a children's book:

"The Beavers and the children didn't know what to do or say when they saw him. People...sometimes think that a thing cannot be good and terrible at the same time...when they tried to look at Aslan's face they just caught a glimpse of the golden mane

and the great, royal, solemn, overwhelming eyes; and then they found they couldn't look at him and went all trembly."

Their reaction is reminiscent of the Apostle John in the book of Revelation. John son of Zebedee is called the beloved disciple. He saw Christ in person as a young man and had served Him all his life well into his old age. John had seen Christ tired and hungry and thirsty. Seen His sorrow and His compassion. When confronted by the Sanhedrin to stop preaching, he declared with Peter:

"Whether it is right in the sight of God to listen to you rather than to God, you must judge, for we cannot but speak of what we have seen and heard." --Acts 4:19b-20, ESV

Tradition tells us the Apostle John was even on the Isle of Patmos in exile after the Roman Empire failed to kill him by throwing him in a vat of boiling oil. This was a man who knew Christ deeply and followed him with zeal and fervent love. But when he saw Christ in the vision as He really is, John was terrified.

"and in the midst of the lampstands one like a son of man, clothed with a long robe and with a golden sash around His chest. The hairs of His head were white, like white wool, like snow. His eyes were like a flame of fire, His feet were like burnished bronze, refined in a furnace, and His voice was like the roar of many waters. In His right hand He held seven stars, from His mouth came a sharp two-edged sword, and His face was like the sun shining in full strength.

When I saw Him, I fell at His feet as though dead." -- Revelation 1:13-17

That's the same sort of reaction as the prophets of the Old Testament who saw God, and it's what we really need to recognize about God. He's not a cloud or genie or bit of candy to pass our fancy. He's good, but He's sovereign. He's gentle, but omnipotent. He calls us but not to safety in this world. He is everything we should want and absolutely deserving of a well-reasoned fear. "God is love" but He is also "a consuming fire" (1 John 4:8, Hebrews 12:29, ESV). The key is, like the Pevensies, we must seek Him out all the same. Whether He is "safe" or not is immaterial. He is good and rules by right and once we accept that and approach in that manner all His gentleness, His radiant warmth, and kindness will become apparent. Especially if we are willing to follow Him wherever He leads.

The Horse and His Boy

When I first read *The Lion, The Witch, and the Wardrobe*, I wondered something. Why did Aslan leave the children in Narnia so long? Years passed. They grew up and reigned in splendor:

"These two Kings and two Queens governed Narnia well, and long and happy was their reign... And Peter became a tall and deep-chested man and a great warrior, and he was called King Peter the Magnificent. And Susan grew into a tall and gracious woman with black hair that fell almost to her feet and the kings of the countries beyond the sea began to send ambassadors asking for her hand in marriage. And she was called Queen Susan the Gentle. Edmund was a graver and quieter man than Peter, and great in council and judgment. He was called King Edmund the Just. But as for Lucy, she was always gay and golden-haired, and all princes in those parts desired her to be their Queen, and her own people called her Queen Lucy the Valiant."

They lived almost full lives in Narnia. Part of it was sure to be it helped create stability for Narnians escaping the White Witch's century long rule. Certainly, it is possible their time was a reward for their service, but when considering another book in the series, *A Horse and His Boy*, I start to wonder if there was more. Something else we might glean.

In *The Horse and His Boy*, the Pevensies are nearing the end to their resplendent rule of Narnia--though they don't know it. Edmund and Susan, effectively adults now, intersect the story while on a diplomatic visit to Calormen's capital city, Tashbaan.

Though heroes of the first book and eventually seen with almost Arthurian reverence by later Narnians, King Edmund the Just and Queen Susan the Gentle weren't the focus of this story. You might point out that's obvious. But think about it. As important as they are being rulers of Narnia and protagonists of other books, their role in this story was to help Shasta, Aravis,

Bree, and Hwin. They weren't protagonists but supporting characters. Part of Aslan's bigger plan. Sometimes I think we forget that we too are vessels of the Lord's creation. He doesn't bless us just for our own benefit. We're to give freely because we received freely. (Matthew 10:8) Our blessings may in turn be a much-needed help for others the Lord loves dearly and our role in events supportive, marginal.

Consider also that the Narnians as a whole were benefitted by the Pevensies' reign. They had peace and prosperity after their long hardship under the White Witch. The four kids remained long enough to help bring healing to the land. To help build hope in their subjects' hearts. That hope saw Narnia through more than a thousand years and the oppressive rule of the Telmarines. Likewise, we may not understand the impact of our lives and the purpose of all the good we receive till much later. Long after we've yielded to the Lord's will and allowed ourselves to be used to aid others He loves and for whom He has plans.

Whether our roles in events and life appear significant at the time or not, we must never lose sight of the bigger picture. God is over it all and working all things out in accordance with His will. We can be certain that working for His purposes creates the very best story for our lives possible.

Heal the sick, raise the dead, cleanse lepers, cast out demons. You received without paying; give without pay. – Matthew 10:8, ESV

Prince Caspian

"The Lord is not slow to fulfill his promise as some count slowness, but is patient toward you, not wishing that any should perish, but that all should reach repentance." -- 2 Peter 3:9, ESV

As a fan of history, I really enjoy it when fictional stories show two different time periods in the same world. I'm doing that in the *Quest of Fire Saga*, and a big inspiration for how to tell a story of that sort is C. S. Lewis's *Prince Caspian*. It features the world of Narnia which looks vastly different from what the Pevensies left at the end of *The Lion, The Witch, and the Wardrobe*.

Without going into too many details, over a thousand Narnian years have passed and the events the Pevensies out are now legend. Narnia's most fantastical creatures live in oppression or hide in hopes of overthrowing a despotic ruler from the human Telmarines. The titular hero is the rightful heir of Telmar, but sides with the Narnians in large part because he believes in Aslan. That fact actually proves to be such an interesting part of the story, because so many of the Narnians don't. In the hardship of the centuries since Aslan returned to life and overthrew the White Witch, the voices who rose over the din are mostly cynical ones.

"What do you think, Trumpkin?" asked Caspian.

"...your Majesty knows I think the Horn—and that bit of broken stone over there—and your great King Peter—and your Lion Aslan—are all eggs in moonshine... All I insist on is that the army is told nothing about it. There's no good raising hopes of magical help which (as I think) are sure to be disappointed."

Caspian almost gives up on Aslan and entertains other counsel till it takes him to the dark place of contemplating necromancy and calling up the White Witch. He's only rescued from the danger doubt had allowed to creep into his life by the very deliverers he and the others doubted.

The world is trying to tell us all the time that we can't be serious about following Christ. Saying things like, "If God were real He would've shown Himself by now." We're told to grow up and find something new to believe in. To accept there is nothing marvelous about this world other than its complete lack of marvel.

"...scoffers will come in the last days with scoffing, following their own sinful desires. They will say, "Where is the promise of His coming? For ever since the fathers fell asleep, all things are continuing as they were from the beginning of creation."
-- 1 Peter 2:3-4, ESV

Caspian and the Narnians weren't the only doubters in the book. Lucy was treated like she was crazy when she told her siblings she could see Aslan and they couldn't. It was a struggle to convince them otherwise, particularly for the dwarf Trumpkin who didn't believe Aslan or the Pevensies even existed:

"I did wonder if there really was such a person as Aslan: but then sometimes I wondered if there were really people like you. Yet there you are."

Christ is real and He will come. Hold on to your faith. It is true, "we walk by faith not by sight." (2 Corinthians 5:7) But remember, "faith is the assurance of things hoped for, the conviction of things not seen." (Hebrews 11:1) Don't forget Who God is and what He is like and when the world challenges us for our "silly, kiddish" beliefs we'll stand firm because we know the Truth.

The Voyage of the Dawn Treader

Throughout *The Chronicles of Narnia*, C. S. Lewis frequently pulled in creatures and characters from his favorite myths and legends. This included nymphs, dryads, Father Time, the Greek god Bacchus, satyrs, and mermaids. Obviously some additions were more contentious with Christian readers than others--ahem, Bacchus. Usually these additions make tiny ripples in the story, giving color and depth to the world of Narnia without begging too many questions. There is one major exception for me. Though Bacchus raised my eyebrows when I read *Prince Caspian*, it was the inclusion of the merkingdom near the world's end during *The Voyage of the Dawn Treader* that pulled me up to a hard stop.

For some context, the book focuses on a sea-faring journey of exploration by Caspian, now firmly King of Narnia, Edmund, Lucy, and their cousin, Eustace Scrubb. By the time the merkingdom appears beneath the waves, they've already sailed leagues beyond anything charted and were almost to the edge of Narnia's world. So, this undersea civilization was only ever seen and interacted with by Caspian's expedition. This drew me up short, because Aslan obviously made them and they were intelligent creatures, but why make them only to be alone save for one brief passing like ships in the night? This begs questions of things in our own world. Why did God create such an immense universe? Why are there entire ecosystems buried beneath the deepest parts of the oceans that we have scarce discovered or microscopic ecosystems with a dizzying array of species? There are things in Creation that no one would ever see apart from the most powerful telescopes, microscopes, etc. There are many more things we may never see in Creation's present state and many things we may have missed altogether.

As someone who really likes to have solid reasoning behind what I believe, I pondered on those questions for a while. This is effectively the conclusion I came to:

"Oh, the depth of the riches and wisdom and knowledge of God! How unsearchable are His judgments and how inscrutable His ways!" -- Romans 11:33, ESV

I think God's conversation with Job in the final chapters of that book make a potent case for this. God points out His creative works and challenged Job to tell Him where Job was during all of it. Consider also God's purposes in bringing Israel into Egypt and then out in the Exodus. It was to display His glory to the world. Scripture frequently points out that Israel wasn't chosen for its own righteousness, but rather because they were such underdogs against wicked forces in the world that it underscored how great God is. God's creative works are beyond comprehension. His Creation isn't just for our benefit or use; it is for His pleasure and His glory.

Pause to digest that idea. It's a really humbling notion that though we're the centerpiece of His Creation, we aren't the focus. God is the focus and meaning behind all that exists and that should help us keep the right view of Him. He's infinite, holy, indescribably glorious, and to degrees and in ways we have yet to fathom.

We may one day see much more if the restored creation is open to our exploration, like finding the lost realms of the seas or microscopic world. Perhaps God will grant us insight into all the annals of history past to reveal things buried by the ages. We may even be permitted to peer into the depths of the universe and comprehend its vastness. Regardless of what we can or ever will see of it all:

"The heavens declare the glory of God, and the sky above proclaims His handiwork. Day to day pours out speech, and night to night reveals knowledge." -- Psalm 19:1-2

Considering Lewis's high view of God's creativity and nature, I think it's no coincidence that he once said, "Don't use words too big for the subject. Don't say 'infinitely' when you mean 'very'; otherwise you'll have no word left when you want to talk about something really infinite." In God we find true infinity, and every positive word of the greatest potency, scope, and praise falls pitifully short.

The Silver Chair

"So it's no good, Pole. I know what you were thinking because I was thinking the same. You were thinking how nice it would have been if Aslan hadn't put the instructions on the stones of the ruined city till after we'd passed it. And then it would have been his fault, not ours…No. We must just own up. We've only four signs to go by, and we've muffed the first three."

In this scene the trio of Eustace Scrubb, Jill Pole, and Puddleglum the Marshwiggle are discussing how they failed to identify a sign Aslan had given them in the quest to find the long-lost prince, Rilian. Aslan had given Jill four signs to memorize and look for along the way.

"…let nothing turn your mind from following the signs…Here on the mountain, the air is clear and your mind is clear, as you drop down in Narnia, the air will thicken. Take great care that it does not confuse your mind. And the signs which you have learned here will not look at all as you expect them to look, when you meet them there. That is why it is so important to know them by heart and pay no attention to appearances. Remember the signs and believe the signs. Nothing else matters."

Jill did not recognize the first sign and missed an opportunity to make their work easier. Their second and third failures were tied in large part to the group being tired and cold. Circumstances stole every bit of their attention away and they decided to go to Harfang Castle instead of looking for the signs. The promise of a warm bed and meal at Harfang turned out to be a deadly trap which they only just escape.

So, by the time they encounter the fourth sign, *"You will know the lost prince (if you find him) by this, that he will be the first person you have met in your travels who will ask you to do something in my name, in the name of Aslan,"* the trio was at last hyper-aware of the signs. They were looking actively, though once again they found themselves facing a predicament. The one asking something of them was a knight under an enchantment who had just warned them that at a certain time of night he becomes possessed and will turn into a giant serpent if left unbound. At the appointed time he did change, but it was into his real self--or so he tells them--and asks them in Aslan's name to free him. Suffice it to say, they struggled with this request.

There's something interesting at this point in the story. As they're discussing what to do, it becomes apparent to Puddleglum that they have to trust the sign they were given. If they don't and this proves to be the sign, they've failed. If they do and it isn't the sign, they will be killed. Moreover, Narnia will lose its rightful future king and could face disastrous strife. For us, the consequences of following God's signs, that is the pathway outlined in Scripture for living our lives, is fraught with choices of a similar kind. In the West, we rarely face life-or-death outcomes of a physical sense, but the spiritual consequences of continually choosing to misinterpret, ignore, or reject the signs we're shown are dire. Consider Ezekiel 33:1-7:

"The word of the LORD came to me:'Son of man, speak to your people and say to them, If I bring the sword upon a land, and the people of the land take a man from among them, and make him their watchman, and if he sees the sword coming upon the land and blows the trumpet and warns the people, then if anyone who hears the sound of the trumpet does not take warning, and the sword comes and takes him away, his blood shall be upon his own head. He heard the sound of the trumpet and did not take warning; his blood shall be upon himself. But if he had taken warning, he would have saved his life. But if the watchman sees the sword coming and does not blow the trumpet, so that the people are not warned, and the sword comes and takes any one of them, that person is taken away in his iniquity, but his blood I will require at the watchman's hand.

'So you, son of man, I have made a watchman for the house of Israel. Whenever you hear a word from my mouth, you shall give them warning from me.'"

Some theologians debate whether these words are directly applicable to Christians or simply to the Old Testament prophet, Ezekiel. The debate of personal judgment for our silence aside, we are called to be a light in this world (Matthew 5:14). If we value all Scripture as instructive to us for our present lives (1 Corinthians 10:11), then we must take seriously the notion that our obedience to all the signs we find in life can impact our lives and this world for the worse or the better.

If you've never read how *The Silver Chair* ends, I encourage you to dig into it and find out whether they free the knight or not. As you do, in addition to all the other great morsels of truth found in those passages, remember, God gave us His Word:

"But as for you, continue in what you have learned and have firmly believed, knowing from whom you learned it and how from childhood you have been acquainted with the sacred writings, which are able to make you wise for salvation through faith in Christ Jesus. All Scripture is breathed out by God and profitable for teaching, for reproof, for correction, and for training in righteousness, that the man of God may be complete, equipped for every good work." – 1 Timothy 3:14-17, ESV

Never stop meditating on and looking for God's signs in your life.

The Last Battle

At the close of *The Chronicles of Narnia*, C. S. Lewis gives us an interesting perspective embedded in a pair of scenes that tell us the most important things about God, and ourselves, yet. The first comes with the dwarfs tossed into the stable where the demonic creature Tash was said to reside. They were fortunate enough to be imprisoned there after Tash had been cast out by Peter Pevensie, but they were miserable. We quickly discover their misery is self-imposed. Lucy tries to get Aslan to comfort them, so he provides them good food and drinks and improves their surroundings, but they don't see it. Which prompts Aslan to comment, *"Dearest...I will show you both what I can, and what I cannot do."* Aslan is Christ in Narnia, and we know He has no limits, so why would Aslan say that? Because God has chosen to do something truly marvelous in order to cultivate real love. He has chosen not to exert His will in irresistible manner. This is the tragedy of free will. We can be the dwarfs who "have chosen cunning instead of belief" to our harm.

In contrast to this, we see later all the Pevensies farther in and further up in Aslan's Country talking to Aslan. They don't want him to send them back to England again, they want to stay in Narnia. At this point, Aslan reveals that an earlier incident involving the train they were all riding on in England had a crash. They were all killed. That seems like a very somber and tragic way to close out *The Chronicles of Narnia*, but Lewis's tone isn't sad. It's joyful, hopeful, and exuberant. The Pevensies don't cry. They are swept up in wonder, because they've reached the goal of it all. Their choice was Aslan, was Christ, and everything that follows after is shown to be better than anything before. It is the reality of which they had only before seen shadows

"For now we see in a mirror dimly, but then face to face. Now I know in part; then I shall know fully, even as I have been fully known." -- 1 Corinthians 13:11-12, ESV

By this point, every Narnian has passed one of two ways. The choice was represented by a single file line streaming up to a door in which stood Aslan. When a Narnian saw him they either loved him or hated him. Including those dwarfs that refused to believe anything whose *"prison is only in their own minds...and so afraid of being taken in that they cannot be taken out."* I think Lewis was getting at something key to understanding the choice God puts before us. It's not about us gaining Heaven or Hell as much as it is about us choosing Christ. Loving Him, or not. There are consequences to our choice, gently reflected in *The Last Battle*. The ultimate purpose, though, is restoration of what we always should have had, what we were made for. Belief, obedience, and love are all intertwined and represented in the life of a Christian. Likewise if Adam and Eve had believed God in Eden, they would have obeyed and that obedience would have revealed their love's truth. Lewis famously said in his World War II radio chats, later collected in Mere Christianity, *"When the author walks on to the stage the play is over...what is the good of saying you are on His side then, when you see the whole natural universe melting away like a dream and something else--something it never entered your head to conceive--comes crashing in; something so beautiful to some of us and so terrible to others that none of us will have any choice left? For this time it will be God without disguise; something so overwhelming that it will strike either irresistible love or irresistible horror into every creature."*

God's love is such that we get what we want, even if it is an insult to Him, and grieves His heart:

"The Lord is not slow to fulfill his promise as some count slowness, but is patient toward you, not wishing that any should perish, but that all should reach repentance." -- 2 Peter 3:9, ESV

We tend to see things very much from our local view. Things now are of imminent importance, we expect a Happily Ever

After here and now. But Lewis closes his Narnia series with a powerful reminder that our real Happily Ever After is Christ and that is what He and we have been searching for all along. The choice now to believe results in an obedient love that finds its greatest fulfillment when we are finally with Him without shadows, veils, or distractions. When we too shall see things as the Pevensies and heroes of Narnia did:

"Now at last they were beginning Chapter One of the Great Story which no one on earth has read: which goes on forever: in which every chapter is better than the one before."

Author Bio - Brett Armstrong

Brett grew up hearing whispers of fantastical books set in a land called Narnia but didn't brave their adventures till he was an adult. Now he frequently makes return visits to them, relishing the beauty of the paradoxical combination of simplicity and depth. He regularly draws from them for lessons in life and fiction writing as he seeks to infuse his own work with the same beautiful paradox of simply-told deep truth.

Brett Armstrong has been exploring other worlds as a writer since age nine. Years later, he still writes, but now invites others along on his excursions. He's shown readers hauntingly sorrowful historical fiction (*Destitutio Quod Remissio*), scary-real dystopian sci-fi (*Tomorrow's Edge Trilogy*), and dark, sweeping epic fantasy (*Quest of Fire* saga). Where he heads next is as much a discovery for him as readers. Through dark, despair, light, joy, and everything in between, the end is always meant to leave his fellow literary explorers with wonder and hope. *https://brettarmstrong.net*

About
The Quest of
Fire saga

A true tale of fantasy threatens to consume a teen's world. Jason is an expert at running from his past. But when it catches up, he finds himself hiding in a peculiar inn and listening to a tale from centuries past.

The story is Anargen's: a teen who is pulled from all he loves to follow his oaths of loyalty to the fabled King of the Realms. Together with his mentor, Cinaed, he rides north on a special quest to mediate peace talks between ancient foes--the men of Ecthelowall and the dwarfs of Ordumair. Nothing goes as planned. Many on both sides of the dispute despise Anargen's Order. Worse, an arcane evil has returned to the North. This "Grey Scourge" seeks to ruin the peace talks and ensure a lost treasure held by the dwarfs is never found by those for whom it is meant.

As Anargen's story unfolds, Jason begins to wonder whether it is truly just a fable. He soon finds himself drawn into the conflict Anargen faced. A battle which has shaped and can destroy his world.

Myths and Folly

One of humanity's traits that seems to transcend location and era is the mythologizing of events. Whether it's retelling a story of a crazy camping trip, regaling listeners with past sports victories, or relating events in the life of an American Founding Father, we as human beings have a tendency to tell stories with embellishments. That's unfortunate, because many fully true stories are far more incredible than the fabricated ones.

A byproduct of our legend building is that we develop a level of skepticism towards truly incredible happenings. We shield ourselves from disappointment by refusing to be "taken in". When you combine that with our tendency to forget things, even important things, we have the recipe for something like what troubles the Lowlands in *Quest of Fire: The Gathering Dark*. In Anargen's era of that world's history, the High King is already beginning to be viewed as a relic of the past. A far past figure with embellishments something like George Washington seems to modern Americans. His actions and decrees don't impact day to day living and only matter to a diminishing number of loyal Knights.

Hundreds of years later in the book, Jason lives at a time when the High King is viewed as a mythic figure, more akin to King Arthur. When Jason meets the storyteller in the Black River Inn who begins talking about the High King and a quest his knights went on in the past, Jason almost writes it off, except the storyteller relates the tale as truth. Most listeners laugh at him and tell jokes about the looney old man. He really believes it happened and acts that way. A local councilman threatens the storyteller with severe consequences if he doesn't stop telling the tale, but the storyteller continues anyway. This really piques Jason's interest.

When relating events from Scripture it's important to not waver in our own conviction. We aren't telling embellishments or half-truths (2 Peter 1:16). Scripture warns that as world history draws to a close, people are going to be skeptical. They aren't going to take us seriously. They'll laugh us off or try to silence us. But we can't shrink back in fear (Hebrews 10:38-39). It shouldn't surprise us that as western culture becomes more secular and open to pagan ideals, skepticism towards Christianity is growing. Didn't the Greeks and Jews to whom the message was first delivered react the same way?

"For the word of the cross is folly to those who are perishing, but to us who are being saved it is the power of God. For it is written, 'I will destroy the wisdom of the wise, and the discernment of the discerning I will thwart.'...For Jews demand signs and Greeks seek wisdom, but we preach Christ crucified, a stumbling block to Jews and folly to Gentiles, but to those who are called, both Jews and Greeks, Christ the power of God and the wisdom of God." -- 1 Corinthians 1:18-19, 22-24, ESV

Like many in the past, we have seen a great light (Isaiah 9:2) and are looking for a city with eternal foundations. A land to which this world cannot compare (Hebrews 11:10, 1 Corinthians 2:9). We should live and share the Truth in such a way that others pause to consider the depth of conviction we possess.

"You will be hated by all for my name's sake. But not a hair of your head will perish. By your endurance you will gain your lives." -- Luke 21:17-19, ESV

You never know who will be drawn to the Truth by your conviction and endurance.

Brothers by Proxy

Sometimes people feel like giving up. As a writer, there are days I just want to close my laptop and move on. We can get worn down and frustrated, especially in relationships. I've had my share of disputes and grudges over the years. It's all too easy to become bitter and distant when someone does something that wounds us. To sever ties with the person and just give up on it. It feels like there's no road back at times. I know that's been true for me, particularly in one case.

Growing up an only child, my closest friends and I were brothers by proxy. One of my friends in particular. He was there the night I accepted Christ as my Savior, and he raised his hand as well. We played on the high school soccer team together and hung out each day after school. We played street basketball, watched all of prequel and original Star Wars movies, and majored in the same subject at college. For the first year at college we were roommates, so I got to see him reading C. S. Lewis and other works that he informed me were something called *apologetics*. That was the first time I had encountered the word. It was an undeniable influence on getting me interested in the field of study.

You can probably guess that our friendship hit rocky straits. It's still in them. I would like to say that I'm daily working to mend things, but that wouldn't be true. The desire is there, but acting on it feels like moving a mountain.

A scene in *The Gathering Dark* features one of the protagonists, Anargen, meeting his mentor Cinaed after being parted for a time. When he does, his initial joy is cut down as he realizes Cinaed might not be who he thought he was, nor his deeds as chivalrous as he'd like to believe. In fact, he's pretty sure Cinaed has secretly allied himself with the men of Ecthelowall who were doing their level best to wipe Anargen, the Knights, and Ordumair off the map. Anargen has a crisis of confidence and is torn over

38

what to do. Circumstances made Cinaed seem sinister, but was there actually some good behind it all? Anargen feels so despondent. How is he to reconcile what he sees with what he knows of Cinaed?

There are moments when those we admire, those who are like brothers to us, will do things that break our hearts. I don't know that I will ever see my friend in the same way again. There are times when we cannot continue as we have in the past. But one thing we never do is give up hope. Hope for the best in those we know, praying continuously as 1 Thessalonians 5:17 instructs us. We pray for everyone, even enemies, but especially for those we care about. The Lord sees the heart where we see only external circumstances:

"For the Lord sees not as man sees: man looks on the outward appearance, but the Lord looks on the heart." -- 1 Samuel 16:7b, ESV

In the course of breaking away from my friend, there were a host of incidents that cast my friend in an unfavorable role of antagonist. But was he really? Sometimes I wonder, if we had the Lord's perspective how many wounds would be seen as accidental and incidental? How many grievances had mutual origins and merit repentance on both sides?

Our sight in this world isn't that clear, unfortunately. That's probably why the Lord told us through the Apostle Paul:

"Love is patient and kind...it is not irritable or resentful... Love bears all things, believes all things, hopes all things, endures all things. Love never ends." -- 1 Corinthians 13:4a,6b-8a, ESV

We are to love even those who hate us (Luke 6:27). Should we be ignorant and oblivious though? I think the answer, without digging too deep in a theological discussion, is again to pray continuously. Let Scripture light our paths and allow the Holy Spirit to lead us into all truth (Psalm 119:105, John 16:13).

I cannot say whether the outcome for Cinaed and my friend are wholly parallel. I don't yet know what the Lord may do in my friend's case. But I can say that, like Anargen I don't allow the scars others inflict on me, intentional or not, to hinder praying for their well-being and hoping the best of and for them.

Diligence

"As for you, always be sober-minded, endure suffering, do the work of an evangelist, fulfill your ministry." -- *2 Timothy 4:5, ESV*

There are several moments in *The Gathering Dark* where Anargen faces the opportunity to turn back from the quest he's on. The choice to leave his home had already cost him the comforts and joys he had always hoped for. He left an easy life well provided for in Black River with his parents and the girl he loved to make the hard journey north. Things go from bad to worse for Anargen and his friends. Anticipated allies prove to be antagonists at best and outright enemies more often. Political forces driven by centuries old grudges threaten to grind them under as supernatural forces converge to destroy everything around them. Even the dwarfs of Ordumair, who hate Anargen's Knight Order, are confused by his diligence and question him.

Each time he is faced with the chance to run, Anargen had to choose to keep on the journey, to keep following the High King even as it seemed to cost more and more. That's us. Christians daily face a similar directive from the King of Kings:

*"And he said to all, "If anyone would come after me, let him deny himself and **take up** his **cross** daily and follow me."* -- *Luke 9:23*

We've died to self once we accept Him but following Him is evidenced in the daily persistence of putting to death our desires that oppose His Word. We may not be called to risk our lives to help those who hate us, but we are instructed to love them. To not speak badly of them. To pray for them and be there when they need help in any of a thousand ways.

"To this end we always pray for you, that our God may make you worthy of his calling and may fulfill every resolve for good and every work of faith by his power, so that the name of our

Lord Jesus may be glorified in you, and you in him, according to the grace of our God and the Lord Jesus Christ." -- 2 Thessalonians 1:11-12, ESV

There are few good things in life that can thrive short of consistent effort being applied. Muscles atrophy in disuse. Neural connections wither if neurons aren't stimulated. I know my art is never as good after a long break from it as when I'm consistently doing sketches. If you think about it, the trend goes further than that. In general, scientists agree that life is characterized by growth, the ability to obtain nourishment, and an organism's ability to respond its environment. Considering God is Creator and so much of the physical world mirrors the spiritual (1 Corinthians 13:12), is it any surprise our spiritual well-being is something that requires continual attention? Stopping well short of suggesting our new life can end--I believe we cannot bring that about (John 10:27-30)--we can certainly fail to live up the high calling we've received. The writer of *The Book of Hebrews* exhorts us:

"Therefore, since we are surrounded by so great a cloud of witnesses, let us also lay aside every weight, and sin which clings so closely, and let us run with endurance the race that is set before us, looking to Jesus, the founder and perfecter of our faith, who for the joy that was set before him endured the cross, despising the shame, and is seated at the right hand of the throne of God. Consider him who endured from sinners such hostility against himself, so that you may not grow weary or fainthearted." -- Hebrews 12:1-3, ESV

Most of us have never had to risk our lives for the faith, but we are all called to the kind of faith that is dedicated, persistent and does not yield under pressure. Anargen lived out his oaths to the High King by pressing on and fighting for the Ords. We live out ours by carrying our cross daily.

Confusion on the Path

I imagine it would surprise some readers to discover authors cringe when writing some scenes. For me in particular, I feel like writing is discovery. It's the act of uncovering a story's paths in advance, trailblazing a road through a story landscape on which readers will follow after. One scene in *The Gathering Dark* was particularly painful. Anargen and his friends are ambushed by highwaymen en route to meet up with Sir Cinaed at the city Abarros. After narrowly escaping the encounter with their lives, there is no way for them to meet up with Cinaed at the appointed time. They feel guilty, because they're sure if they hadn't been bickering and messing around earlier, the encounter with the highwaymen would never have happened. One of the group, Caeserus, suggests they lie about the reason. As he sees it, Cinaed isn't above suspicion and has been keeping things from them. Why should they reveal that their immaturity had caused the delay? Particularly if it jeopardized their chances to participate in such an important quest. It hurt to write the scene because I knew all four teens were going to choose wrongly.

We do not suffer from an overabundance of trust and faith and understanding. We live in an era of skepticism, doubt, and suspicion. Like the dwarfs of C. S. Lewis's *The Last Battle* we would rather live in prisons of disbelief rather than accept truths that are discordant to our own narratives.

The danger is that this tendency towards self-reliance and outward skepticism leaves us vulnerable when real truth tries to speak to us. Anargen and his friends knew what the right thing to do was. It wasn't a mystery. But circumstances and the suspicion of others led him to join in the group deception. Disaster waited at the end.

"There is a way that seems right to a man, but its end is the way to death." -- Proverbs 14:12, 16:25, ESV

The citation above isn't an error. Both Proverbs 14:12 and 16:25 say exactly, Hebrew word for Hebrew word, the same thing. The author of the verses, and certainly God, was trying to make something very clear to us. Our judgment is compromised and should be questioned. The Bible gets at it another, gentler way:

"All we like sheep have gone astray; we have turned every one to his own way; and the Lord hath laid on Him the iniquity of us all." -- Isaiah 53:10, ESV

We know the Him Isaiah 53:10 ultimately refers to is Christ just as surely as we can understand that the every one that has gone astray includes you and me. That is why it is so crucial to stay grounded in the Scriptures to make sound decisions.

"All Scripture is breathed out by God and profitable for teaching, for reproof, for correction, and for training in righteousness, that the man of God may be complete, equipped for every good work." 2 Timothy 3:16-17, ESV

We, who have a corrupt and darkened world obscuring our view of the right path to travel, consider David's proclamation:

"Your word is a lamp to my feet and a light to my path." -- Psalm 119:105, ESV

When we question what the right way to go might be, we must turn to Scripture. Of course, the immediate tendency is to protest, "Well what about things not explicitly in Scripture? How can we know what Scripture teaches then?" While writing this entry, these verses spoke loudly to me:

"When the Spirit of truth comes, He will guide you into all the truth, for He will not speak on His own authority, but whatever He hears He will speak, and He will declare to you the things that are to come. He will glorify me, for He will take what is mine and declare it to you. All that the Father has is mine; therefore I said that He will take what is mine and declare it to you." -- John 16:13-15, ESV

We can't trust ourselves; we make wrong choices. We need Scripture, God's Word. To understand God's Word and will, we need the Holy Spirit. Easy. Actual practice, much like proving any theorem, is far removed in terms of experienced difficulty from that ease. Once again we can allow circumstances to cloud our decisions. But then again, following Christ has never been about ease, it's about honoring the one true God. Christ warned His disciples, and through them us:

"I have said these things to you, that in me you may have peace. In the world you will have tribulation. But take heart; I have overcome the world." -- John 16:33, ESV

Victory

"'I have come where the High King sent me,' Anargen responded with conviction.'I do not know why the Grey Scourge is here, only how. Where there is no light, things of the dark need not skulk. They are free to be brazen and cruel. Your land has been without light for a long time.'

'You came to die then, hungerman?' another Ord asked, his voice cracking." -- Quest of Fire: The Gathering Dark

The excerpt above occurs while the teen protagonist Anargen is trapped in the fortress with the dwarfs defending it. The enemy is slowly pushing their backs to a wall, figuratively and literally. It doesn't look good. Anargen left his home, the girl he loved, and the ease of life and honor most Knights enjoyed in Black River. The surrounding dwarfs, and Anargen himself, wondered why he would've been sent to them only to fail. Which begs the question, does God ever allow us to fail in what He commands us to do?

"For to me to live is Christ, and to die is gain." -- Philippians 1:21, ESV

The Apostle Paul might have wondered the same thing. He certainly was justified to. His letter to the believers in Philippi came during years following God's will and preaching the Good News of Christ. He had seen great miracles and escaped death numerous times. But at the end of his life, he was in jail. Not only that but the Emperor Nero had decided to pin the fire that destroyed a third of Rome on Christians. Nero is said to have burned Christians alive to serve as torches along streets. Paul himself was set to be executed. What did he say about all that?

"For I am already being poured out as a drink offering, and the time of my departure has come. I have fought the good

fight, I have finished the race, I have kept the faith." -- 2 Timothy 4:6-7, ESV

Paul was beheaded sometime after penning those words. I don't think he died believing he'd failed, though Nero certainly would've told him that and pretty much anyone observing at the time would have likely thought he had failed too. But I doubt Paul saw it that way and history certainly gives a far different perspective, even by worldly standards.

We don't always know why God has placed us in the circumstances He has or why we're suffering a "defeat". It isn't ours to know. What we can know is God will never leave us nor forsake us (Hebrews 13:5). Whatever happens around us, we have to keep our eyes on our Savior. Where He leads is where we need to be and from whence true good may come.

Never give up the fight of the faith, even when you feel you've lost. Anargen concluded something similar.

"Sometimes we are called to make a stand, even if it ends in sorrow. Sometimes it is the stand which is the most powerful implement for the High King to cast off darkness...Live or die, the light I carried here with me will shine the brighter for what I do now."

The Apostle Paul went on to add:

"Henceforth there is laid up for me the crown of righteousness, which the Lord, the righteous judge, will award to me on that day, and not only to me but also to all who have loved his appearing."-- 2 Timothy 4:8, ESV

The victory is never about what we perceive, but what the Lord has done and will do. His is the victory, the glory, and the honor forevermore. A forevermore we are privileged to participate in that is worth holding fast to.

Author Bio - Brett Armstrong

Brett grew up hearing whispers of fantastical books set in a land called Narnia but didn't brave their adventures till he was an adult. Now he frequently makes return visits to them, relishing the beauty of the paradoxical combination of simplicity and depth. He regularly draws from them for lessons in life and fiction writing as he seeks to infuse his own work with the same beautiful paradox of simply-told deep truth.

Brett Armstrong has been exploring other worlds as a writer since age nine. Years later, he still writes, but now invites others along on his excursions. He's shown readers hauntingly sorrowful historical fiction (*Destitutio Quod Remissio*), scary-real dystopian sci-fi (*Tomorrow's Edge Trilogy*), and dark, sweeping epic fantasy (*Quest of Fire* saga). Where he heads next is as much a discovery for him as readers. Through dark, despair, light, joy, and everything in between, the end is always meant to leave his fellow literary explorers with wonder and hope. *https://brettarmstrong.net*

About
The Lord of the Rings

The Lord of the Rings is an epic high fantasy series of books written by J. R. R. Tolkien. It could be said that this is the definitive work of fantasy written and released in the last century. Its impact has a far and broad reach, laying out plot structures and themes that would inspire and be emulated by many writers for a nearly a century after its initial writing, and it will continue to do so for the foreseeable future.

Tolkien's work has had such broad impact that it has inspired new words in the Oxford English Dictionary and inspired generations of art, film, video and board games, music, and practically every other medium. In 2003 it was named Britain's best novel of all time.

It is nearly impossible for a fan of fantasy, science fiction, or pop culture to escape the impact of Tolkien's work. The Lord of the Rings continues to be one of the best-selling novels ever written.

Middle-Earth: Fiction that Parallels Reality

Depending on who you listen to, Middle Earth, the setting of J. R. R. Tolkien's Lord of the Rings epic, has a few origins. According to an interview with the author, it has parallels within Norse mythology's Midgard (where humans live). Within the greater legendarium of the stories, the prime locations (a place called Endor,) were surrounded by a greater landmass named Beleriand during the first age, but it was flooded as that era ended with the fall of Numenor.

If you are unfamiliar with Numenor, they were a people group. Numenor was the greatest civilization of mankind. They worshipped the One God (named Iluvatar in Tolkien's mythos, described as the single omniscient and omnipotent creator,) and were a great race.

Sauron rose to power in Mordor (yes, the same very villain we see trying to destroy mankind in the Lord of the Rings.) He claimed to be the ruler and king of mankind. The Greatest Race took issue with that--and Sauron quickly found himself confronted with a military force of Numenorians who Sauron knew he could not defeat. Sauron is a Valar, or Ainur, a race of powerful spirit creatures one step above the Maia, (pseudo-angelic beings who include Gandalf and other wizards and creatures--as well as the balrogs.) The Maia were divine, but their immortality had limits: they could be killed.

Sauron tricked the Numenorians by surrendering and they took him as a prisoner where he rose to power from within as an adviser to King Ar-Pharazôn. Numenor eventually rebelled against the Valar and grew increasingly wicked before attacking the Undying Lands (something similar to Heaven), the home of the Valar and of Iluvatar's chief representative.

While faithful Elendil and his sons fled wicked Numenor in ships, Iluvatar destroyed Numenor with a great flood that recast the landscape for the future. In doing so, He reshaped the world and made it so mortal men can no longer sail west and arrive in Valinor by their own efforts.

Christian inspiration is written all over this one.

Fast forward to the fourth age. We now have hobbits on the scene, though not as populous as elves and dwarves. Mankind is widespread, and those rare descendants of Elendil (including Aragorn, the rightful king of Gondor,) are also amongst them. Goblins, orcs, and other twisted and corrupt creatures now roam the land, too, while Sauron works from the shadows to cast his evil across the land.

Gandalf discovers the thing that anchors his evil in the realm of men: a magic ring. He seeks to destroy it, along with several other heroes from a mixed company of the races. By now, Sauron's evil influence has spread into even the other maia and Gandalf no longer knows who he can trust.

He places that trust in the nontypical hero. Frodo isn't a hero at all; he is a hobbit, a little person from a quiet countryside where battles and adventures are a rare and foreign thing. Frodo doesn't really even want to go on such a quest... but a call is given, and he responds with a willingness, even if reluctantly.

Frodo didn't get a vacation. His journey was arduous and deadly. He was kidnapped, chased by orcs, lost, nearly drowned in the marshes, poisoned by a giant spider, and sought with evil intent at every turn. He did not know his strengths--and he felt the weight of his limitations. Neither were his primary concern, only answering the call.

The call of a believer comes much the same. Our mission is to seek and save the lost while being a representation of Christ's love before all mankind. Have you seen mankind? We're not exactly sunshine and roses; we often have more in common with unlovable goblins than with nobler races. Still, the call remains. Christians can only fulfill our calling through sacrifice.

Sacrifice is more than a verb.

Looking at Lord of the Rings from the 10,000 foot level, it becomes more and more evident that, sometimes, *we must be* the sacrifice. Likely, we could all likely recite a verse about dying to ourselves, picking up crosses, etc. Sometimes we are called to do more than merely *make* sacrifices... rather we might be called to *be sacrifices*. This is a daunting idea that necessitates we surrender our basic rights: the right to be heard, the right for presence and attention, the right to be angry, the right to autonomy. A living sacrifice has no rights other than to die on behalf of others.

Romans 12:1 NIV Therefore, I urge you, brothers and sisters, in view of God's mercy, to offer your bodies as a living sacrifice, holy and pleasing to God--this is your true and proper worship.

Giving up rights seems unfathomable--especially to people from Western cultures. American and European mentalities hardly understand sacrifice any longer; we barely understand the difference between inconveniences and martyrdom! Our rights are so ingrained in the fabric of our psyche, but the rest of the world does not play those same rules.

Believers obey a different law; believers have a higher calling and a greater command. We are representatives from a greater place than where we currently live and work. We are *ambassadors* for that kingdom. *2 Corinthians 5:20 NIV says We are therefore Christ's ambassadors, as though God were making his appeal through us. We implore you on Christ's behalf: Be reconciled to God.*

Christians have been "approved by God to be entrusted with the gospel" (1 Thessalonians 2:4) and are called to an epic journey through this world--this life, even while not belonging to it (John 17:16). Our mission is to call as many others as we can to journey alongside us and join our Fellowship. Put in those terms, it's easy to identify with Gandalf, Frodo, or any other member of Tolkien's Fellowship.

Whether hobbit, dwarf, or other, the call is the same. Even poor Gollum was called to the adventure; our fates all tied up in it. It is an adventure worth taking. As Tolkien wrote, "It's a dangerous business, Frodo, going out your door. You step onto the road, and if you don't keep your feet, there's no knowing where you might be swept off to," and such is the nature of a Christian's call.

When God calls you to it, do you accept his journey, or do you remain in your comfortable hobbit hole?

Brothers and sisters, think of what you were when you were called. Not many of you were wise by human standards; not many were influential; not many were of noble birth. 1 Corinthians 1:26 NIV

As a prisoner for the Lord, then, I urge you to live a life worthy of the calling you have received. Ephesians 4:1 NIV

Tolkien: The Storyteller's Story

John Ronald Reuel Tolkien was born in Bloemfontein, South Africa, on January 3, 1892. They returned to England three years later after J.R.R.'s father fell ill with rheumatic fever. Shortly after, his father died. Less than a decade later, when J.R.R. was only twelve, he became an orphan with the passing of his mother.

Despite his mother's background as a Baptist, Mabel Tolkien became a Roman Catholic in 1900 and, despite being a single-parent widow, Mabel's family cut off all financial assistance. Four years later she would be dead. Before passing, Mabel assigned his guardianship to her friend, Father Francis Xavier Morgan.

At the age of sixteen, Tolkien met a girl, Edith Mary Bratt; she was three years older than J.R.R. Both she and he were orphans and very like-minded. Father Francis discovered their love when the teenage J.R.R. grades dipped; he forbade the relationship until J.R.R. was twenty-one years old. Grades were one thing, but J.R.R. was a Catholic and Edith was a protestant and the priest hoped that the passage of time might quell their affections. For the most part, J.R.R. honored Father Francis's demand.

On his twenty-first birthday J.R.R. wrote to Edith and declared that he never stopped loving her despite the silence. She was engaged to another at this point--a relationship which she broke off for J.R.R. At this discovery, Bratt's guardian and benefactor broke with her and evicted Edith. The young lovers made it work and married anyway.

Later, less than a decade after World War I, he would go on to teach at Oxford where he was an alum. He lost most of his friends to the bloody war, which he spent much of in an infirmary after contracting trench fever, a similar circumstance to his friend C. S. Lewis, who also taught at Oxford.

Lewis was known for some criticism of his friend, citing J.R.R. as a bad lecturer with something of a mild speech impediment. One gets the sense of J.R.R.'s story that he endured incredible hardships through his life--most of these circumstances came from outside factors, either in the form of tragedy such as his parent's untimely deaths, or as other people's circumstances or choices directly impacted him.

It may have felt at times that the entire world was against poor J. R. R. Tolkien. But regardless of that, he remained true--and even obedient to the point of remaining in silence for four years away from the great love of his life (and perhaps one of the great love stories of the last century. Their relationship formed the basis of Beren and Luthien story: the pair of lovers upon which much of the Lord of the Rings background is founded on—but more on that later.)

Tolkien was faithful, and it was his faith that carried him through. He relied on it--possibly recalling God's promise in Jeremiah 1:19. *"They will fight against you but will not overcome you, for I am with you and will rescue you," declares the LORD.*

Perhaps your life feels much the same: like nothing is going right. Things are maybe difficult, slow, bogged down in minutia, or others have set fires to every bridge that you have built. This was Tolkien's same situation. He endured, and became one of the most widely-read authors of our age. He endured, not because of the stories that drove him, but because of his faith.

Here is God's promise in the Psalms (25:1-5, 20-21 NIV).
In you, Lord my God, I put my trust.
I trust in you; do not let me be put to shame,
nor let my enemies triumph over me.
No one who hopes in you
will ever be put to shame,
but shame will come on those
who are treacherous without cause.
Show me your ways, Lord,

teach me your paths.
Guide me in your truth and teach me,
for you are God my Savior,
and my hope is in you all day long.

Guard my life and rescue me;
do not let me be put to shame,
for I take refuge in you.
May integrity and uprightness protect me,
because my hope, Lord, is in you.

The Fourth Age

"In a hole in the ground there lived a hobbit."

The Hobbit

The Lord of the Rings is richly built and contains several eras' worth of lore. Tolkien was a language expert and made up entire countries, civilizations, and thousands of years' worth of background data during which to tell his stories. He made up the word "hobbit," and both Bilbo and Frodo Baggins' unexpected journeys take place during a period of time known as the Fourth Age.

Hobbits have no mention in Tolkien lore before the Third Age. While their origins are never discussed, J.R.R.'S son speculates some, suggesting that the Northmen and Rohirrim remember tales of them, and that they lived in the Vales of Anduin in Wilderland, between Mirkwood and the Misty Mountains at that time.

While still in the Valley of the Anduin River, the Hobbits grew uneasy because of the growing numbers of men from the East who passed the Greenwood and harassed the Northmen. They, too, likely sensed the rising Shadow of Dol Guldur as evil powers rose again in the too-close distance. The little folk took up the arduous task of crossing the Misty Mountains and journeyed westward. Eventually they came to a land between the River Brandywine and the Weather Hills. Eventually they crossed the Brandywine and into the Shire proper, settling into the quiet, peaceful people we discover them to be in The Hobbit and in The Lord of the Rings.

Remaining for many generations in the Shire, hobbits live idyllic lives. Wars and conflict are known to them, but they remain far-off, foreign things. Hobbits understand that evil exists, but it is not close enough to be anything more than a passing threat.

Whenever danger is discussed, it is quickly discounted, often as being "someone else's problem."

Many believers have a similar mentality to hobbits. Their spiritual life revolves around an event, experience, or their conversion which happened many years prior. Complacency creeps in. Church life becomes comfortable. Spiritual battle is far removed; money is given to missionaries who are sent to the front lines. Money goes to them because the pagans, muslims, atheists, etc. *would never come here...* and we have built our faith communities so that *they never* could *come here.*

"Oh there was a battle once. Old Bullroarer Took sent those goblins packing. Killed their leader--knocked his head clean off! No more goblins around here, my friend. They'll never return. We are safe in the Shire... anyone else in trouble must have gone looking for it... that's why we stay here, *in our nice, comfortable holes.*" Most hobbits live in the past; danger is not something that can touch them if they refuse to think about it, like children pulling blankets over their heads to hide from monsters in the closet. But evil comes calling anyway. Evil found Frodo in the tranquility of his home. Ringwraiths invaded the Shire.

Alternatively, there are Christians who, like the rest of those in Middle Earth, long to see *more* than evil simply removed from their midst. They want to see evil *conquered* and to see the proper king restored to His throne. These believers are willing to take up swords and fight at the request of the King.

In Judges we find the story of Gideon. His story seems to bridge both mentalities. The Midianites invaded and destroyed harvests every year. Israel hid in caves and restructured their communities, content to eke out whatever living they could--never daring to challenge the evil that harried their land.

In Judges 6:11-16 we find Gideon's call as he's doing farm work in hiding. God tells him how it is the King who will win this battle for him. He merely need be obedient to the call.

The angel of the Lord came and sat down under the oak in Ophrah that belonged to Joash the Abiezrite, where his son Gideon was threshing wheat in a winepress to keep it from the Midianites. When the angel of the Lord appeared to Gideon, he said, "The Lord is with you, mighty warrior."

"Pardon me, my lord," Gideon replied, "but if the Lord is with us, why has all this happened to us? Where are all his wonders that our ancestors told us about when they said, 'Did not the Lord bring us up out of Egypt?' But now the Lord has abandoned us and given us into the hand of Midian."

The Lord turned to him and said, "Go in the strength you have and save Israel out of Midian's hand. Am I not sending you?"

"Pardon me, my lord," Gideon replied, "but how can I save Israel? My clan is the weakest in Manasseh, and I am the least in my family."

The Lord answered, "I will be with you, and you will strike down all the Midianites, leaving none alive."

Are you a content hobbit, satisfied to leave the action to others, though the battle rages on your borders? Or are you someone who longs for the return of the King and will march under His banner?

How might God be calling you to adventure beyond the comfortable Shires of your life?

Tolkien and Lewis: Rise of the Inklings

After teaching for about a year at Oxford's Merton College, Tolkien met a fellow professor named C. S. Lewis at a faculty meeting. They didn't leap into a fast friendship straight away, but eventually bonded over a love of Norse mythology.

Tolkien was a strong believer, and at that time (as well as it is now,) it was popular among professors and college students to voice their outspoken opposition to Christian faith. At the time of their meeting, Lewis was an outspoken atheist, having left behind a heritage of faith at age seventeen.

Despite the religious difference, Tolkien and Lewis worked on their own projects and tolerated each other's idiosyncrasies. After a few years, recognizing the lack of quality sci-fi and fantasy, they formed a literary society together named The Inklings. During their early friendship, Tolkien is credited with defending his faith to his friend on multiple occasions.

Through this period, Tolkien was writing some of his earlier material which created the foundations for Middle Earth; he'd been working on the epic love story of Beren and Luthien. Lewis encouraged him to continue mapping out his universe. Lewis was perhaps Tolkien's only source of encouragement and even after the original publication of the Hobbit and Lord of the Rings, Tolkien wasn't recognize as much more than a language professor who wrote dragon and wizard stories.

Tolkien wrote in a letter to Dick Plotz, "Thain" of the Tolkien Society of America, in 1965. "[Lewis] was for long my only audience. Only from him did I ever get the idea that my 'stuff' could be more than a private hobby. But for his interest and unceasing eagerness for more I should never have brought The Lord of the Rings to a conclusion."

During that early writing period, Lewis experienced his own crisis of faith, or non-faith as it was; his ardent belief that God was a lie seemed in jeopardy when he thought about it critically. The Spirit worked on Lewis's heart. While Lewis battled with thoughts and feelings he struggled to comprehend, he called himself the "most dejected and reluctant convert in all of England."

One fall evening in 1931, Lewis took a walk with Tolkien and another fellow Inkling, and by dawn he had decided to convert to Christianity. A renewed faith sparked Lewis's imagination, and he began to weave Christian themes into his writing. Lewis pushed Tolkien to bring his fantasy world to life on the page as well. Tolkien would later write, "The unpayable debt that I owe to [Lewis] was not 'influence' as it is ordinarily understood but sheer encouragement."

Without Lewis, the writings of J. R. R. Tolkien might have never made it beyond stacks of dusty notepads. Without Tolkien we might not have C. S. Lewis and his diligent apologetic works. Without Tolkien's ambition to evangelize his friends, Lewis might not have found a relationship with Jesus.

Interestingly, the two did not even get along at first. They made it a point to find something in common and then work together to influence each other's lives positively.

> *To the weak I became weak, to win the weak. I have become all things to all people so that by all possible means I might save some. I do all this for the sake of the gospel, that I may share in its blessings. 1 Corinthians 9:22-23 NIV*

Lewis said, "What Tolkien showed me was this: that if I met the idea of sacrifice in a pagan story, I didn't mind it at all. I was mysteriously moved by it. The reason was that in pagan stories, I was prepared to feel the myth as profound. Now the story of Christ is simply a *true myth*."

Beren and Luthien

It is interesting how closely the tale of Beren and Luthien intertwines with the biggest aspects of Tolkien's faith and life. The story of these star-crossed lovers was foundational to the Middle Earth mythos, and also part of C. S. Lewis's faith story (Lewis was Tolkien's lone voice of encouragement,) as well as a parallel to J.R.R.'s love story with Edith Mary Bratt.

Like his romance with Ms. Bratt, the elf maiden Luthien was prohibited from marrying the human Beren by Luthien's father, Thingol. Thingol set an impossible task for Beren to accomplish and prove he was worthy of marrying Luthien: to steal one of the three Silmaril gems from the crown of Morgoth (Sauron's master). If you thought Sauron was tough, he had nothing on Morgoth.

Beren and Luthien both work towards this goal, undeterred by others. When Beren is taken hostage by Sauron, Luthien comes to his aide. When Beren will not be deterred to abandon his quest, others surround him and accompany him on his journey. Beren even sacrifices his own hand for this purpose as he and Luthien flee from Morgoth's stronghold at Angband.

Much like cyclical stories within scripture (the cycles of judges is a famous one among others) there are patterns within great works of writing: stories often hearken back to greater tropes that foreshadowed great truths. Beren and Luthien is a cornerstone of Middle Earth. While it is not necessary reading, and Aragorn and Arwen's love story is great, knowing Beren and Luthien is a key to going deeper into the thinking of these two characters whose fates interweave through the struggles of man against evil— and even more amazing, it is a shadow copy of the very author's great love for his wife (Luthien's first meeting of Beren is based on a real rendezvous between Tolkien and Bratt.)

There are many romances contained within scripture. Ruth and Boaz, Abraham and Sarah, and Song of Solomon come readily to mind, among others. In many ways the romance story of Tolkien and Bratt hearkens back to Jacob and Rachel. Tolkien's guardian, when learning of the romance with Bratt, forbade contact until Tolkien was twenty-one years old.

Jacob fell in love with Rachel and sought her hand. Rachel's father Laban insisted that Jacob work for him seven years and then he would permit the marriage. Jacob agrees, but Laban tricks Jacob and veils the bride--who he switched at the last minute for Leah, Rachel's older sister. The marriage is complete and vows are given by the time Jacob realizes the trick. Laban insists that he work another seven years in exchange for Rachel's hand. Jacob agrees to complete what might seem like an impossible task.

Jacob, Tolkien, and Beren were each taken with true love--not some passing moment of lust. They obeyed the conditions set out by their authorities; they honored vows and committed wholly to completing difficult tasks to gain the object of their desire.

Jesus talks about gaining a valuable treasure and being willing to pay the high cost to obtain it. In his Parable of the Hidden Treasure Jesus speaks to the willingness to sacrifice *all* in order to obtain a thing.

> *"The kingdom of heaven is like treasure hidden in a field. When a man found it, he hid it again, and then in his joy went and sold all he had and bought that field." Matthew 13:44 NIV*

Jesus is speaking about heaven in this brief parable, but the principle of the thing is true. If you are committed to something great (whether it's a romance, a valuable item, or an achievement,) no obstacle should stand in your way. Fling yourself into battle against the impossible odds and find a way to overcome for the sake of the reward.

What is your impossible task? What is it worth to accomplish victory? Maybe it's not a romantic endeavor that you are striving for. It might be a spiritual objective; it might be raising your child in the faith--or maybe it's a passion to share Jesus with a friend (such as Tolkien did with C. S. Lewis.) Whatever it is, commit to it--figuratively *sell all that you have* in order to see your goal accomplished. May the God of Love and Wisdom guide you in your efforts as you strive to claim your own Silmaril.

Who is Aragorn

"I am Aragorn son of Arathorn, and am called Elessar, the Elfstone, Dúnadan, the heir of Isildur Elendil's son of Gondor."
The Two Towers

When the hobbits first met him, he went by the name Strider. Aragorn has a long history and has many names, as is often the case for prominent kings.

That Tolkien wrote with biblical parallels is no secret, and he wrote very Christological themes into the character of Aragorn: the person who was simply a man, but was also the rightful king. While not a true allegory, readers of Lord of the Rings gain a familiarity with concepts that we see embodied in the person of Jesus.

Aragorn lived in obscurity. He had the ability to heal. He had power over the dead and led them in a great battle. He was a long-desired king who was promised to restore a languishing kingdom.

As a ranger of the North, Aragorn lived in obscurity and never sought the glory that was due him. He is a character torn by his desire to do what's right and a fear of fulfilling his destiny. Tolkien describes Aragorn as an average person--probably the type of man you could meet and quickly forget--whereas rulers like Boromir, the son of the Steward of Gondor (the acting ruler) wore fine clothes and was accustomed to the recognition and esteem of his peers. Tolkien put it, "All that is gold does not glitter," to describe Aragorn's "plainness."

Likewise, Jesus is spoken of prophetically in Isaiah 53:2, *He had no beauty or majesty to attract us to him, nothing in his appearance that we should desire him.*

Aragorn was a healer-king.

Some have speculated that Aragorn's healing powers increased as he began to step confidently into the role that had been prepared for him: to assume the mantle of the King. This would explain why he could not heal Frodo's wound of the Morgul blade in the first book, but could later heal things such as Faramir's arrow wounds, Eowyn's injuries, and Merry the hobbit. If that is that case, which might be a stretch, it parallels the ministry of Jesus who began a ministry of healing after he stepped into his official "ministry role" in the final years of his life that led up to the crucifixion. It might just as well be that he healed more because there was great need of it, or that his confidence was a crucial component that he lacked up until he claimed his rights to the throne. If that is the case, it might be a better conclusion to see a commission for us to bring healing as well.

In Luke 10 Jesus sent out seventy-two disciples to confidently preach and heal in his name.

After this the Lord appointed seventy-two others and sent them two by two ahead of him to every town and place where he was about to go. He told them, "The harvest is plentiful, but the workers are few. Ask the Lord of the harvest, therefore, to send out workers into his harvest field. Go! I am sending you out like lambs among wolves. Do not take a purse or bag or sandals...

"When you enter a town and are welcomed, eat what is offered to you. Heal the sick who are there and tell them, 'The kingdom of God has come near to you...'

"Whoever listens to you listens to me; whoever rejects you rejects me; but whoever rejects me rejects him who sent me." The seventy-two returned with joy and said, "Lord, even the demons submit to us in your name."

He replied, "I saw Satan fall like lightning from heaven. I have given you authority to trample on snakes and scorpions and to overcome all the power of the enemy; nothing will harm you. However, do not rejoice that the spirits submit to you, but rejoice that your names are written in heaven."

Aragorn has the power to release the dead from their curse. He proves this after he enters the Path of the Dead and summons the deceased traitors from the mountain to fulfill their ancient oath and fight for Gondor. He willingly entered the realm of the dead and proved that he had all authority over it.

Not only did he set the captives free from the power of the grave, but Aragorn redeemed those in the bondage of death's curse. In Tolkien's story, Aragorn released them from a curse--released them from their hell--in Scripture, the truth is so much more profound--we are not merely rescued from the fires of Hell, but we are saved to a life in service of such a great King who would do battle on our behalf. The passage from Luke reiterates this: *I have given you authority to ...overcome all the power of the enemy... However, do not rejoice that the spirits submit to you, but rejoice that your names are written in heaven."*

Would you have been one of the seventy-two? That same commission from Luke 10 applies to us today: it is the mandate of every believer. Jesus is sending us out in his name to be healers and preachers in the world: to reclaim a kingdom that teeters on the brink.

Aragorn is a great example of what and who we are to be, so walk in His name and power, and claim the royal lineage you were born for.

Being Boromir

Boromir is the son of Denethor II (who is the sort of an intermediary king called a Steward.) Denethor always favored Boromir over Faramir, his younger brother. Even so, there was no animosity between them. Because of his skill and prowess, Boromir was made Captain of the White Tower and quickly became Captain-General; at a young age he gained the title High Warden of the White Tower. He led many successful campaigns against Sauron's forces.

Both brothers received visions as a summons to the council of Elrond, though Faramir saw them first. Boromir journeyed to Rivendell and joined the Fellowship as the representative of the human race, making his part in the story something of an Everyman tale.

As the heir to his father's position as ruler of Gondor (at least until the king returned to claim the throne and rule,) he is fiercely concerned for the welfare of his country. During the Fellowship's quest, the thoughts that he could use the One Ring as a weapon on behalf of his people tempted him. For all of his strength in battle and physical ability, Boromir succumbs to the corruption of evil and he betrays Frodo, attempting to take the ring by force.

Overcome by both his internal conviction and by the words of Aragorn, Boromir was sent to look after Merry and Pippin when the sudden appearance of orcs during the search for Frodo scattered the party. They repelled the orcs, but the vicious uruk hai came next and Boromir defended them with his life. He fought to the death for their protection and spoke words before his death that showed his genuine repentance for his failure with Frodo. He died something of a martyr's death.

Boromir was so strong in some areas, and yet so weak in others. Much like Boromir, we too have chinks in our armor. His desperation to save his country drove him to betray his companions with his attempt to seize the Ring. He joined the Fellowship in a genuine effort to stamp out evil and answer the call that he felt in his spirit. Somewhere along the way, that true calling shifted on its axis and became trumped by his patriotism.

This is especially common in Western politics and faith. I'll say it again for the political-minded Christians in the back: Boromir let his patriotism force his spiritual calling to play second fiddle.

In many circles, patriotism has become synonymous with faith culture. This is a dangerous slope, and it affects both sides of party aisles. God calls us to become citizens of a higher kingdom... *His* Kingdom. The calling to follow Jesus is a calling to become an ambassador of Christ to a lost and fallen world. We should not be a vassal of Gondor to the rest of Middle Earth--but a member of the *higher calling*, a Fellowship that fights evil everywhere rather than merely propping up one faction or country (or political party).

We are each like Boromir. We have all, at some point, failed (Romans 3:23 for all have sinned and fall short of the glory of God.) Every one of us is called to repentance and to holy works as we walk out our faith; Phillipians 2:12b-13 *continue to work out your salvation with fear and trembling, for it is God who works in you to will and to act according to his purpose.* The Greek verb rendered as "work out" means "to continually work to bring something to completion or fruition." We do this by actively pursuing obedience as God sanctifies us.

The first time I read LOTR I was very young, and I didn't fully understand the position of Steward of Gondor, the role Denethor filled and which Boromir would inherit. The first time it finally made sense to me was when I read the Parable of the Talents in Matthew 25:14-30.

"For it will be like a man going on a journey, who called his servants and entrusted to them his property. To one he gave five talents, to another two, to another one, to each according to

his ability. Then he went away. He who had received the five talents went at once and traded with them, and he made five talents more. So also he who had the two talents made two talents more. But he who had received the one talent went and dug in the ground and hid his master's money. Now after a long time the master of those servants came and settled accounts with them… he who had the two talents came forward, saying, 'Master, you delivered to me two talents; here, I have made two talents more.' His master said to him, 'Well done, good and faithful servant. You have been faithful over a little; I will set you over much. Enter into the joy of your master.' He who had received the one talent came forward, saying, 'Master, I knew you to be a hard man, reaping where you did not sow, and gathering where you scattered no seed, so I was afraid, and I went and hid your talent in the ground. Here, you have what is yours.' But his master answered him, 'You wicked and slothful servant! You knew [all of this] Then you ought to have invested my money with the bankers, and at my coming I should have received what was my own with interest."

In our King's absence, we are called to steward the Kingdom and to do so rightly and justly. Boromir and Denethor are both examples of stewards who failed to live up to the King's desires. As modern Boromirs we must take care not to make the kingdom around us into something it is not; nor should we entirely hide our allegiance and fail to cultivate its increase. This is not an easy position; if it was easy, we would all be wildly successful in this endeavor.

Boromir was a multifaceted character. For all his faults, he was bold even in his failing and he admitted his mistakes, repented, and worked to fix his errors.

It's probably too late to tell you not to be like Boromir. But if you find yourself *starting* to behave like Boromir, try to *finish* like Boromir.

Did Frodo Wear Sneakers?

"...they were a merry folk. They dressed in bright colours, being notably fond of yellow and green; but they seldom wore shoes, since their feet had tough leathery soles and were clad in a thick curling hair, much like the hair of their heads, which was commonly brown."

Concerning Hobbits
(Fellowship of the Rings Prologue)

Tolkien nerds might be quick to point out things from the film series that aren't necessarily story-canon. The size of Hobbit feet is a hot topic on Tolkien forums, (Tolkien never said they were over-sized and he never stated that the Shire-folk did not wear shoes... only that they *seldom* did.) Granted, the visual media of cinema works best for them to have the features established by Peter Jackson's special effects team.

There exists a wealth of information written by J. R. R. Tolkien by way of interviews and letters. Letter 27 states that *"There is in the text no mention of his acquiring of boots. There should be! It has dropped out somehow or other in the various revisions – the bootings occurred at Rivendell; and he was again bootless after leaving Rivendell on the way home."* Straight from the author himself: Bilbo wore boots/shoes. At least, he could have.

I don't often wear great shoes. Except for a couple pairs of boots that I own, I tend to buy the cheaper options and they wear out sooner than those of my peers. Still, the thought of a hobbit wearing sneakers (regardless of size) is a little absurd, though it reminds me of another funny movie scene. Marty McFly wears a pair of Nike sneakers in the old west in Back to the Future 3. "What's that writin' mean... Nee-Kay?" asked one cowboy.

Nike is the Greek goddess who personified victory. The verb form of Nike means "Absolute, conquer, prevail in battle, in the games, or in any contest; prevail, be superior." It presupposes conflict or rivalry and is used in the Greek New Testament twenty-eight times (and nearly as many in the Septuagint, the Greek version of the Old Testament). Biblically, it is most often translated as *overcome*.

Interestingly, as a verb, *nikao* is not simply something that happens in a vacuum. It hearkens back to the noun form, *nike*. It calls upon a power, translating as "victory, the power that provides victory." Without a form of power to enable defeating the opponent, victory could not be expected. Overcoming was not possible without a source of power.

Frodo was an overcomer; he had a great villain he needed to defeat, but he had no power. Frodo undertook on this journey knowing that he did not have the strength to overcome the challenges it would present. Gandalf, a great source of wisdom, notes[1] that, "It is not the strength of the body that counts, but the strength of the spirit." Even at Frodo's weakest moments, he decides to see the journey through until its end--understanding that it will require him to sacrifice his life in order to overcome this enemy. As believers in Christ, we have access to a "power that provides victory," that is the Holy Spirit--the personified aspect of power who is the third member of the Trinity (that literally translates as the root word for dynamite—now that's power!)

Like Frodo, we are also in a war--a war against sin and evil, not altogether different than the battle for Middle Earth, although more spiritual in nature. We must remember that the world is a battleground, not a playground. Overcomers are not sinless, but hold fast to faith in Christ until the end. He or she does not fall away when times get difficult, they stand firm. Overcoming requires complete dependence upon God for direction, purpose,

---

[1] *This is a line attributed to Gandalf in a film-based calendar but was not written by Tolkien and it did not make it into the final cut of the film.*

fulfillment, and strength to follow His plan for our lives--that is the power that the Holy Spirit provides.

We need to become Ring-bearers; like Frodo we carry a weighty load of evil that we must bear but ever resist. The Bible calls us cross-bearers, bearing the burden of evils in the world and their destructive consequences, and all without becoming Ring-wearers, like the Nazgul, men who were corrupted and became the wicked servants of evil, slaves to the power of the world.

This is how we know that we love the children of God: by loving God and carrying out his commands. In fact, this is love for God: to keep his commands. And his commands are not burdensome, for everyone born of God overcomes the world. This is the victory that has overcome the world, even our faith. Who is it that overcomes the world? Only the one who believes that Jesus is the Son of God. 1 John 5:2-5

There are really only two options for those of us who are believers. 1. We submit to the powers of evil and wear a ring of temptation, becoming like the ring-wraiths: slaves to the dark power. 2. We resist evil, take up our cross, and move forward under the power of the Holy Spirit; we follow Jesus. Be like Frodo: overcome.

The only power that can enable us to claim the *nike* is the Holy Spirit. We would do well to rely on it.

Shards of Narsil

In that house were harboured the Heirs of Isildur, in childhood and old age, because of the kinship of their blood with Elrond himself, and because he knew in his wisdom that one should come of their line to whom a great part was appointed in the last deeds of that Age. And until that time came the shards of Elendil's sword were given into the keeping of Elrond, when the days of the Dúnedain darkened and they became a wandering people." The Silmarillion

I admit to a certain fascination with swords--especially those with a good deal of history. Nothing evokes the romantic ideas of a great back-story like a broken sword.

In 1991 there was a short-lived cartoon on television called The Pirates of Darkwater. It was ahead of its time, and unfortunately never resolved, but the main character wielded a broken sword that belonged to his father. It's a trope that has been used many times, and borrows from the shattered sword motif that resonates through Tolkien's greater works (it was a broken blade that woke Morgoth as Beren pried a Silmaril free from the evil one's crown and it was a broken blade in the Story of Kullervo that sends the tragic hero over an emotional cliff.)

Narsil was a long sword wielded by the human king Elendil during the War of the Last Alliance. It broke as Elendil died after falling upon it. After his death at the hands of Sauron, his son, Isildur, used it to cut the One Ring from Sauron's hand during the final battle of that war.

Tolkien was not a man to leave critical history out of his notes. We learn through Tolkien's extended works that the sword was forged during the First Age by the Dwarven smith Telchar of Nogrod. In the Second Age, Narsil had become the heirloom of the descendants of Elros, the first King of Númenor. It eventually came into the hands of Elendil, a distant descendant, towards the close of the Second Age and it was with him until he died by Sauron's hand and claimed by Isildur. In the later ambush at the Gladden Fields which took Isildur's life and freed the One Ring into the wild (and is later reclaimed by Gollum), the shards were rescued by Ohtar, Isildur's squire. He took them to Rivendell, where Isildur's son Valandil was fostered. Elrond foretold that the sword would not be forged anew until the One Ring was found again and Sauron returned.

Before the Fellowship of the Ring departed Rivendell on the Quest of the Ring, the shards of Narsil were reforged by the Elves (this point differs from the film) and Aragorn carried it into the battle of Gondor and wields it in the battle of the Black Gate of Mordor and in defense of Gondor, his kingdom. The sword that was broken was reforged and used as the primary sword of King Aragorn.

The broken sword bears many similarities to the fractured nature of mankind. Because of a great conflict with the evil one, it was broken as death entered, and though the blade was still used, it could no longer retain its full, glorious potential.

Just like Narsil, we are a thing meant to be glorious, but which has been fractured in some cosmic catastrophe. Our nature is broken and we are slaves to sin, rather than bearing the full image of God. We think sinfully, feel, and choose sinfully. Mankind naturally loves darkness (John 3:19), and we do not understand the things of God (1 Corinthians 2:14). The human condition is one of utter lostness (Isaiah 53:6). We are all broken things in need of restoration.

The good news of Christ is that we are made new! Redeemed and repaired with a restored purpose and renewed name.

"Very bright was that sword when it was made whole again; the light of the sun shone redly in it, and the light of the moon shone cold, and its edge was hard and keen. And Aragorn

gave it a new name and called it Andúril, Flame of the West." Fellowship of the Ring

All throughout the Bible we see examples of this--often commemorated by someone receiving a new name. In Genesis we meet Jacob, the younger twin of two brothers. His name translates to something like Usurper/Supplanter.

God has a habit of changing names to match a person's changing destiny. Jacob was changed to Overcomer. Sarah was changed to Princess (it previously meant Argumentative), Peter to Rock, Saul to Paul, Joseph to Barnabas, and there are more. One cannot have a true encounter with the Living God and walk away unchanged (or limp away, as in Jacob's case.)

This is God's promise to us, *"I will give him... a new name written on the stone which no one knows but he who receives it... I will write on him the name of My God, and the name of the city of My God, the new Jerusalem, which comes down out of heaven from My God, and My new name." (Revelation 2:17; 3:12)*

If you are a believer and a follower of Christ, God has given you a name as well. God's grace changes everything about us! When we accept Him, we are made new; we no longer identify with the person we were, but transformed into the likeness of Christ. Like Narsil, the broken nature of mankind is restored to perfection as we are dedicated in service of the true King. Your name, like Anduril's, is changed and you are made into something greater than you ever were before.

The Suffering of Frodo

"It's like in the great stories, Mr. Frodo. The ones that really mattered. Full of darkness and danger they were. And sometimes you didn't want to know the end... because how could the end be happy? How could the world go back to the way it was when so much bad had happened?"

The Two Towers

Everyone loves a good adventure, right? That's part of why we love to read (or consume stories in other ways such as film, or video games.) I love the scene from the first Hobbit movie (the Jackson ones) where Bilbo is running through the Shire yelling, "I'm going on an adventure!" But not all adventures are fun, comfortable affairs. Most are not, in fact.

Living out a faith in Jesus (what we call Christianity) is more of an adventure than it is a decision, a label, a lifestyle, or anything else. Following Jesus means we have a relationship with Him and journey alongside of Him. We have, in effect, joined his company.

Whether we're discussing a life marked by Christ or one that is completely secular, life is hard. Christianity does not promise a life of ease. Rather, it promises redemption and eternal life. However difficult a person's life is will depend on his or her circumstances and calling, not a yes/no checklist about church membership, baptism records, or responses to altar calls or decisions to follow Jesus.

Becoming a Christian does not fix your situations. Unfortunately, somewhere along the way popular religious figureheads shifted into marketing mode and began to sugarcoat the truths of the faith, pitching it as an easy, joyous, and successful alternative to a "secular" existence.

Christianity is often presented as an escape mechanism, a crutch, a way to easily avoid the harsh realities of life. This is a modern fallacy enabled by modern comforts. True faith is the exact opposite--it's a journey that embraces Truth and confronts the world in brave, honest and difficult ways.

Frodo's hardships have sometimes been compared to the suffering of believers, martyrs, Christ, and so much more as people try to find overt Christian threads or lessons within Tolkien's books. We should not shoehorn Frodo's experiences into a box that looks like the brand of religious experiences people prefer. The truth may be far simpler: all life is difficult and fraught with danger. We all fail and endure pain as we struggle against evil-- even the secular person--due to the curse of sin established in Genesis.

Instead of a "nice Christian story" as you'd typically find upon the stores at Christian bookstores, wherein we'd see Frodo return home after a victory and be restored, we find that Frodo does not overcome. He succumbs to evil in the end and becomes corrupted. He suffers permanent physical injury and feels the weight of guilt; his resulting aloofness makes him something of a recluse among his people until he finally leaves with the last elves.

Frodo is a failure. But that's okay. God uses failures and broken things; walking out true faith is impossible without God's constant help. Abraham was elderly. Jacob was a liar. Gideon was a coward. Rahab was a prostitute. David was an adulterer. Job looked like a colossal failure. Samson was a womanizer. Moses had a speech impediment. Paul was a murderer. Martha was a worrier. Lazarus was dead. But God is more powerful than your failings. Failure does not mean that evil wins--it means that we are still as we've always been: in need of God's help.

For some readers, this list of biblical failures might cause despair. It reminds us that we will never be free from the hardships of life. Instead, it should encourage us: God can work in even the worst of humanity and transform us, and our lives, into something glorious and redeemed for His purpose.

And we know that in all things God works for the good of those who love him, who have been called according to his purpose. Romans 8:28 NIV

Do not be surprised at the fiery ordeal that has come on you to test you, as though something strange were happening to you. But rejoice inasmuch as you participate in the sufferings of Christ, so that you may be overjoyed when his glory is revealed. If you are insulted because of the name of Christ, you are blessed, for the Spirit of glory and of God rests on you... if you suffer as a Christian, do not be ashamed, but praise God that you bear that name. 1 Peter 4:12-16 NIV

The fact is, becoming a Christian doesn't always cure sicknesses, repair broken relationships, or improve income and social standing. Troubles don't always disappear when Jesus shows up. Still, following Him is worth it. It has moments of deep joy and blessing and also demands sacrifice and dedication. Practicing humility, patience, and compassion are not easy things, but they are worth it.

A victorious Christian life does not release us from the bad things of life (including natural consequences of our actions or those of others.) But it does establish something even greater in it: the perfect, eternal love of God which operates in and through us.

Perhaps you feel like you've been losing the battle lately. You might have even given up and admitted defeat, but recommitting your way to Christ is perhaps what you need. God is called a *shelter* in Scripture; He will help you ride out the storms and see you through to the next phase of life. Suffering is not eternal. God promises that *He will wipe every tear from their eyes. There will be no more death or mourning or crying or pain, for the old order of things has passed away. (Revelation 2:14) NIV*

The top of this devotional entry starts with a quote from Sam. It is best to let Samwise finish his quote. *"How could the world go back to the way it was when so much bad had happened? But in the end, it's only a passing thing... this shadow. Even darkness must pass."* So, too, will whatever situations and hardships hinder your life.

Who is the True Hero of LOTR?

"His love for Frodo rose above all other thoughts, and forgetting his peril he cried aloud: 'I'm coming Mr. Frodo!'"
Return of the King

Lord of the Rings is, at its base, a hero story. With its myriad of characters, each with different struggles and moral underpinnings, one asks, who is the hero in Lord of the Rings?

Many people would be quick to add their favorite character. Aragorn is an obvious choice. Frodo is, as well. Gandalf clearly displays heroism--even if he, as a Maia, has arguably less at stake than those who dwell on Middle Earth.

Frodo asks what power an insignificant hobbit might have when facing all the potential peril of such a dangerous plan to destroy the One Ring. The enemy is so powerful and overwhelming. And who is more insignificant than Frodo, heir to Bag End and recipient of his uncle's magic ring? *Frodo's gardener*: Samwise Gamgee. He might be the true hero of the Fourth Age.

Sam was more than a good friend; he was a truly loyal companion. Sam saw his place and understood it perhaps more than the other members of the Fellowship: he supported the ring-bearer and his fate was bound to the one he loved. The Bible has many such stories that seem to parallel Sam's loyalty to Frodo. Ruth is one such example.

Ruth 1:16-18 Ruth said, "Do not urge me to leave you or to return from following you. For where you go I will go, and where you lodge I will lodge. Your people shall be my people, and your God my God. Where you die I will die, and there will I be buried. May the Lord do so to me and more also if anything but death parts me from you." And when Naomi saw that she was determined to go with her, she said no more.

But Ruth and Naomi isn't exactly a story about conquering heroes, and Sam seemed to understand that he and Frodo were on a heroes' quest. "It's like in the great stories, Mr. Frodo. The ones that really mattered. Full of darkness and danger they were. And sometimes you didn't want to know the end... because how could the end be happy? How could the world go back to the way it was when so much bad had happened? But in the end, it's only a passing thing... this shadow. Even darkness must pass... I wonder if people will ever say, "Let's hear about Frodo and the Ring." And they'll say, "Yes, that's one of my favorite stories. Frodo was really courageous, wasn't he, Dad?" "Yes, m'boy, the most famousest of hobbits. And that's saying a lot."

Perhaps a better parallel story to Frodo and Samwise would be of David and Jonathan (which can be read in 1 Samuel). Both were bound to each other in a firm friendship--they were close, like a band of brothers. They were both duty-bound to certain courses of actions and even refused the orders of King Saul in order to maintain their honor. Notably, Saul ordered Jonathan to bring David in for execution and Jonathan defied him, while still remaining loyal to his father, the King. David remained faithful to the house of Saul and did not seize the throne from Saul (and Jonathan as the heir) despite having many chances and even though he had been anointed to take that role.

Jonathan and Saul both fell in battle at a later time. This paved the way for David to become king without treachery. If you've read anything about ancient royal succession, (either in history or in fiction books,) it was not uncommon for children and heirs to be killed off by the incoming ruler in order to sever any rival claims to the throne. This was the sad state of reality during that time and was a very real fear.

After learning of Saul and Jonathan's death at the Battle of Mount Gilboa (see 2 Samuel 4) Jonathan's five year old son was snatched by his nursemaid in an attempt to flee and preserve the royal line. The child's name was Mephibosheth and during their flight, he was dropped and injured--crippled so that he could no longer walk and went on to live in secrecy for fear of a hasty execution.

Many years passed and David desired to perform an act of kindness for one of Saul's descendants. He learned about Mephibosheth's existence at that time. Mephibosheth thought he would be killed for his heritage, but David restored his friend's son to a royal inheritance. *"As for Mephibosheth," said the king, "he shall eat at my table like one of the king's sons." (2 Samuel 9:11b).*

David was a biblical hero, for many reasons. Likewise, so was Jonathan. Frodo is one hero in Lord of the Rings--and so is his friend: a simple gardener who refused to give up on his friend despite hardships.

Sam lived in complete obscurity. He viewed himself as weak and second class, but it was the little things like his faithfulness and loyalty that made him the true hero of LOTR. Following the War of the Ring, he stayed behind and lived his life with his family, raised children, etc. Living out the normal expectations of his culture after the adventure makes him someone we can all relate to. *We are all Samwise Gamgee.* We are called to a similar life: to live a normal, common life, but remain poised to answer a sudden call to greatness. This call is based on what/Who dwells inside of us and motivates us to live out our faith daily... all of this means that *YOU* are the hero of Middle Earth, and of all the ages to come.

> *Do not let loyalty and faithfulness forsake you; bind them around your neck, write them on the tablet of your heart. So you will find favor and good repute in the sight of God and of people. – Proverbs 3:3-4 NIV*

Author Bio - Christopher D. Schmitz

Christopher D. Schmitz is author of both Sci-Fi/Fantasy Fiction and Nonfiction books and has been published in both traditional and independent outlets. If you've looked into indie writers of the upper midwest you may have heard his name whispered in dark alleys with an equal mix of respect and disdain. His wife thinks he gets carried away at times. He has been featured on television broadcasts, podcasts, and runs a blog for indie authors... but you've still probably never heard of him.

As an avid consumer of comic books, movies, cartoons, and books (especially sci-fi and fantasy) this child of the 80s basically lived out Stranger Things, but shadowy government agencies won't let him say any more than that. He lives in rural Minnesota with his family where he drinks unsafe amounts of coffee; the caffeine shakes keeps the cold from killing them. In his off-time he plays haunted bagpipes in places of low repute, but that's a story for another time.

You can read more of his stuff, find his mailing list, and more books at *www.authorchristopherdschmitz.com*

About
Wolves of the Tesseract

In a world underneath our own reality, magic & science are two sides of the same coin.

Claire Jones does not normally jump to wild conclusions about the supernatural. Bigfoot, vampires, and the Loch Ness Monster all seemed to have rational reasons... but all of that changes when she is abducted by a shape-shifting hobo and whisked through a dimensional gate. Her captor claims nothing is what it seems, and that a powerful sorcerer believes she is the key to summoning his dark master. Will Claire run from her destiny forever, or can she claim a mythic weapon, and end the sorcerer's reign of terror? Failure releases Sh'logath's cataclysmic power upon the universe.

The Wolves of the Tesseract series is an urban fantasy genre mash-up that pulls from popular themes in YA stories, Lovecraft, and string theory.

Claire as an Everyman

Claire had just barely gotten out of bed; she shook off the comment about her tattered Minnesota Vikings pajama pants, the last gift she'd ever received from her mother before she passed away several years ago.

For all that Claire Jones is or is not, she is something of an *everyman* character. An Everyman is a classic literary type of figure; they are an ordinary individual with whom the audience or reader is supposed to be able to identify easily and who is often placed in extraordinary circumstances.

Claire wants a few things out of her life: happiness, security, family, to love and be loved, and for her life to make sense. She has an especially keen hunger to discover and know the truth of things. It's these things that make her into a sort of everyman.

When she was young, her mother died and she became particularly close to her father, an archaeologist, which meant she wound up on many excavation digs around the world while on her summer vacations. When Claire hears that bigfoot is murdering people in the campgrounds of northland parks near her home, she is driven to investigate. Claire simply can't believe the reports; it doesn't match her worldview.

You may have heard about things like women's intuition, premonitions, etc. I think those ideas stem from our natural (and sometimes supernatural/God-given) discernment. Sometimes you *can just tell when someone is lying* or when something is fake, or fishy. God promises that through the exercise of wisdom we have access to proper discernment. It's not really a supernatural "gift" as much as it is spiritual exercise.

Philippians 1:9 NIV And it is my prayer that your love may abound more and more, with knowledge and all discernment.

Discernment aside, Claire is looking for truth, a parallel to her own spiritual journey as well. She is not an atheist, but neither would someone call her a Believer or a Christian. Claire comments early in the story, "I've seen the collective sum of cross-cultural, historical superstitions and I find it all so... interesting. Not necessarily valid--just interesting. I mean, I believe in *something...* I'm definitely not an atheist. I'm just not entirely certain where the line between reality and fiction intersect."

I've known many, many people like Claire: people who see some truth, but haven't quite embraced it, yet. A lot of those people claim to be Christians, even, though their view of what defines that might not align with scripture.

In all that Claire sees and experiences in the book, she begins to understand that there is much more to life than she realizes. There are things possible in other dimensions and worlds that she never knew existed and where the rules that governed her rigid thinking simply don't apply. Claire had to give up on her nonbelief in order for her life to make sense: there are more powerful forces at work than her rational thinking can contain.

As Claire and Rob flee the Heptobscurantum (cultists who are trying to free a terrifying enemy), she asks questions, still not certain if she's being tricked and kidnapped. She tries to unravel the mysteries of the Tesseract's multi-verse, but could not possibly understand it all at once. At some point, she simply has to operate in what knowledge has been presented and take the rest on faith.

For Claire, that faith was to follow Rob and a test of it was to leap through a portal to another realm where they could hide from the sorcerer Nitthogr's forces. For you and I, the door is quite a bit different: our path to knowing and understanding Truth comes from Scripture and our test is to walk it out in our daily lives.

Sanctify them in the truth; your Word is truth. John 17:17 NIV

To the Jews who had believed him, Jesus said, "If you hold to my teaching, you are really my disciples. Then you will know the truth, and the truth will set you free." John 8:31-32 NIV

Jackie and Claire

Claire matched her giggle. "I don't appreciate being made fun of," she impersonated the flat tone of her fiancé's sister.

Jackie laughed so hard she snorted. She quickly covered her nose; her eyes watered.

There are many levels of friendship. When I was in high school, I had a close-knit group of half a dozen friends or so. Outside of that was another layer of friends who were still good friends… but were tertiary. We didn't share our deepest, darkest secrets, but we might have under some circumstances. Outside of that was a third layer of people who might nowadays be "Facebook Friends," people I was on good terms with, but who were really just one step deeper inside of the circle that I might label "Acquaintances," or simply "people I know."

Jackie and Claire are that first kind: practically sisters. They get each other. If one is having a tough time, the other covers for her and vice versa. They have a mountain of inside jokes and could probably talk in their own made up language composed of movie quotes and facial expressions if absolutely necessary. (It's amazing how often this *is actually necessary* in real life.)

The book of Proverbs gives us so many great pieces of wisdom regarding good and bad friends. Above, Claire and Jackie joke tongue in cheek about a peer they've known for many years and who is about to become Claire's new sister-in-law. Historically she's been a bad friend. That fact doesn't change a whole lot throughout the story. They keep Vivian somewhat at arms-length, being cautious with new friendships. Not everyone *can* or *should* be a close friend. *"A man of many companions may come to ruin, but there is a friend who sticks closer than a brother" (Prov. 18:24).* There is a quality difference in different people and we ought to guard the gates of our heart to make sure that we're not giving the wrong sorts of folks the keys to our inner circle—that close proximity is where the influence is. *Whoever walks with the wise becomes wise, but the companion of fools will suffer harm. Proverbs 13:20 NIV*

Inside that inner circle I feel that there are two types of people that we typically give special access to: those who challenge you as a person or those who you have much in common with. The best of friends will do both. C. S. Lewis said, "Friendship must be about something, even if it were only an enthusiasm for dominoes or white mice. Those who have nothing can share nothing; those who are going nowhere can have no fellow-travelers." Proverbs 27:17 talks about the other kind: those friends who challenge you. *As iron sharpens iron, so one man sharpens another.* Lewis and J. R. R. Tolkien had this sort of dual-natured friendship. They made each other better—often infuriatingly so.

It is a good friend who privately calls you out for living stupidly. There are many different scenarios this might look like: a friend shooting straight with you about a relationship full of problems you are blind to; an accountability partner cautioning you against something; someone being bluntly honest about how you behave at work, etc.

Oscar Wilde famously said, "A true friend stabs you in the front." While Wilde might not be a biblical scholar, there is much truth to his quote. *Better is open rebuke than hidden love. Faithful are the wounds of a friend; profuse are the kisses of an enemy,* according to Proverbs 27:5-6.

Build your friendships around the right things and it will go well for you in life. The cornerstone for a good friendship is mutual faith in God.

"This is my commandment, that you love one another as I have loved you. Greater love has no one than this, that someone lay down his life for his friends. You are my

friends if you do what I [Jesus] command you." John 15:12-14 NIV

The Truth

"Well, what do you think, then?" Claire asked his opinion. "What is really going on?"

"I don't really believe in the impossible, and like Sherlock Holmes said, 'when you have eliminated the impossible, whatever remains, however improbable, must be the truth.'" Professor Jecima paused long as he gave it some thought. "Something supernatural is happening here; not unscientific, just not yet explainable by it."

If anything nowadays, people are desperate for truth but are more confused than ever before. The Bible talks about a coming age of wickedness as the end draws nearer. A resurgence of Babylon's power is part of that, and so is the Spirit of Babel.

I'm not going to get weird on you. The Spirit of Babel is simply a setting of confusion, and just such a spirit pervades our culture. Between social media, biased news outlets with private agendas, political doublespeak, and rampant moral relativism that honors everything except Christ while simultaneously redefining language, the Spirit of Confusion has undeniably permeated our culture. And I didn't even touch on modern viewpoints regarding sexuality, greed, philosophy, or pride.

I read a relevant meme that might mean more to my generation than those younger (I'm from the population at the tail end of Generation X: the last generation to grow up without easy access to technology and the Internet.) The meme read something like, "Remember when we thought lack of intelligence was caused by a lack of information? The invention of the Internet proved that wasn't the problem." It seems that in an age where anyone can learn if anything is true with just the click of a button, *everything and nothing* is true and all at once.

Phrases such as "my truth" have become popular and highlight a culture of relativism: the idea that something that is *true for me* might not be *true for you*. Reality is governed by feelings in this paradigm. Friends, that is not how truth works!

By its nature, truth is absolute. In the movie Forrest Gump there is a scene where Jennie (Forrest's wayward, long-lost love) is high on drugs and standing on a ledge of a building while believing she can fly. Her belief in her ability is very real to her in that moment and she's about to step off. But just because she *feels* she can do it does not make it true. Gravity is the harsh mistress of reality. In our modern paradigm it is no wonder that Christ followers have been villainized--they appear to champion the concrete bellow when they tell the revelers that they should not leap from tall buildings and take to the sky--what narrow-minded, terrible people, right?

Sometimes, to put it bluntly, we *are* the villains. I've known "Christians" who cheer for the concrete rather than rescue the jumper.

Brennan Manning famously said, "The single greatest cause of atheism in the world today is Christians who acknowledge Jesus with their lips and walk out the door and deny Him by their lifestyle. That is what an unbelieving world simply finds unbelievable." The word genuine means "being actually and exactly what is claimed."

For all the confusion in this world, people are pretty good at sniffing out fakes--even if we're equally good at ignoring truth and living in the comfortable, enjoyable fog of half-truths and sugar-coated dreams… but *Christians must be authentic--for the sake of the unbelieving world if not for our own souls!* The atheist philosopher Nietzsche (who famously claimed that God is dead,) said "I might believe in the Redeemer if his followers looked more redeemed."

Ouch. He died in 1900, so this is not a new problem—but does not mean we can ignore they hypocrisy in our midst just because the issue is old. We are called to live genuine lives as much in 1900 or 2099 as much as in the first century when Jesus and His disciples walked and taught on Earth.

So that the tested genuineness of your faith--more precious than gold that perishes though it is tested by fire--may be found to result in praise and glory and honor at the revelation of Jesus Christ. 1 Peter 1:7 NIV

If anyone thinks he is religious and does not bridle his tongue but deceives his heart, this person's religion is worthless. James 1:26 NIV

Today, purpose in your heart to live a true and good life, one that is worthy of the Master's calling.

Daughter of the Architect King

"...It's said that the King offered his life up for all others. That he would remain your hostage for as long as Sh'logath continued to slumber, but that his sons and daughters would forever rule the Prime until he one day reclaims his authority over all creation."

"Why would someone accept those terms," Basilisk retorted. "One life for many? That doesn't make sense... if it happened as you say."

"It does not make sense," Rob agreed. "unless you do value the struggle of life... unless there is still some shred of the old man that still remains: clinging to hope in your original faith--in the old religion of the Prime. Perhaps you were never fully converted to the vyrm ways?"

"And what if I'm not," he snapped at Rob who had obviously touched a nerve.

Behind them, Claire approached the central statue in wonder, taking in the glory of the King.

The story of Claire and her being of royal lineage through no effort of her own is a not so veiled allegory to the "adoption" of believers into the family of God. While Wolf of the Tesseract is admittedly not a perfect allegory, I wanted to add some faith-based parallels to my story (in addition to some wild magic and fantasy unlike anything else I'd encountered... stuff that coincides with some of the more interesting speculations regarding science, multi-verses, and string theory.)

Claire did not realize who she was or could become until she had undergone a transformation of sorts. She realized that there is more to who she is than the simple, basic things she had believed about herself. She begins the story as a relatively passive character full of doubts and disbelief. After discovering who she is, Claire begins to grow in that knowledge and becomes confident enough in what she knows that she continues her fight against the evil sorcerer Nitthogr even after she is separated from her helper, Rob, and is forced to run from Nitthogr's minions.

Claire has an earthly father, but he can't help his dimension-hopping daughter. He couldn't help even if he wasn't fleeing enemies of his own while stuck on Earth. The knowledge that Claire possesses, that she is the daughter of the creator known as the Architect King, brings her comfort even when she is alone, hurt, cold, poor, and pursued.

Much in the same way, we know that we have both earthly family and also a heavenly Father. I understand that not every person has the benefit of having a good father (or having a father at all.) Luckily, Scripture is clear about who He is and how he feels about us. *"See what kind of love the Father has given to us, that we should be called children of God" 1 John 3:1.*

Our Heavenly Father is a rescuer, redeemer, provider, and a true father. When we decide to become a follower of Christ, we become a part of a larger family. Not only are we members of the Church (the family of God--not some building on the edge of town,) but we have a place set aside for us in Heaven--the home that God has prepared for us to one day live with Him.

But when the fullness of time had come, God sent forth his Son, born of woman, born under the law, to redeem those who were under the law, so that we might receive adoption as sons. And because you are sons, God has sent the Spirit of his Son into our hearts, crying, "Abba! Father!" So you are no longer a slave, but a son, and if a son, then an heir through God. Galatians 4:4-7 NIV

The Stone Glaive

...eyeing Claire who took hold of the sword by the excessively long handle. "And then, all your plans and efforts here will have been for naught. The Destroyer will obliterate all existence, the Tesseract will shatter; reality--life--everything will cease, everywhere and all at once!"

Basilisk sighed, staring at Claire who pulled the heavy sword from the hands of the statue, tugging against its weight.

Claire awkwardly locked eyes with Basilisk. "I can take this? I remember only a little of the Prime histories from Bithia."

"You have claim to the sword," the villain said, matter-of-factly.

She snatched the old leather sheathe that lay at the feet of the Architect King and inserted the ancient blade. "Will this help us fight against Nitthogr?"

A common trope in Sci-Fi and Fantasy stories is that of ancient or mythical weapons having immense power against monsters. It is an interesting concept, and one that plays on the idea that the modern generations continually drift away from purer knowledge and wisdoms which were once widely known by our predecessors.

While I certainly think that we have lost some of the things we once knew (or at have least grown apathetic to things we once considered paramount,) it is certainly fact that Western culture has devalued absolute truth and watered down faith-based or religious norms.

Our standard for truth has shifted.

Why is that important to weapons? Because as great as an offense is, we must also consider strong defense in order to be effective in battle. *Truth* is part of our armor and its one the greatest defenses against attacks that a Christian possesses.

Finally, be strong in the Lord and in his mighty power. Put on the full armor of God so that you can take your stand against the devil's schemes. For our struggle is not against flesh and blood, but against the rulers, against the authorities, against the powers of this dark world and against the spiritual forces of evil in the heavenly realms. Therefore put on the full armor of God, so that when the day of evil comes, you may be able to stand your ground, and after you have done everything, to stand. Stand firm then, with the belt of truth buckled around your waist, with the breastplate of righteousness in place, and with your feet fitted with the readiness that comes from the gospel of peace. In addition to all this, take up the shield of faith, with which you can extinguish all the flaming arrows of the evil one. Take the helmet of salvation and the sword of the Spirit, which is the word of God. Ephesians 6:10-17 NIV

Armor is an important part of our defense. Because of the nature of our enemy, we are more likely to need armor than a sword. The only true power Satan has is in falsehood. The enemy will change perception, alter the meaning of things, and twist words to try getting us to abandon Truth.

Without the protection of Truth, we are can neither defend ourselves (defense,) or reclaim what Satan may have taken from us (offense.) Think about it, the first encounter mankind has with the devil is when he lies to Eve and gets her to question the truth of God's command. He offered false promises to Judas making him think that betraying Christ would bring him fulfillment. The liar tried a similar thing with Peter when the disciple tried to prop Jesus up as a political leader, causing Jesus to tell him "get behind me Satan,' pointing out the source of Peter's motivation.

The last thing that the devil wants is a target capable of defense and offense. He much prefers to undo the latches on our armor and leave us naked against his attacks. Because Truth and the Word are intrinsically linked, one cannot last long with only one or the other. If Scripture is not true, we would soon lay down our only effective weapon, and if we believed the lies of the enemy, we would not survive long enough to wield the sword and beat him back.

There is power in speaking and knowing truth, both for defense and also for that fateful day when Christ reclaims the world: when Jesus takes up his weapon and presses a final, definitive offensive and strikes down the wicked by his very Word.

> *And the armies which are in heaven, clothed in fine linen, white and clean, were following Him on white horses. From His mouth comes a sharp sword, so that with it He may strike down the nations, and He will rule them with a rod of iron; and He treads the wine press of the fierce wrath of God, the Almighty. Revelation 19:14,15 NIV*

Author Bio - Christopher D. Schmitz

Christopher D. Schmitz is author of both Sci-Fi/Fantasy Fiction and Nonfiction books and has been published in both traditional and independent outlets. If you've looked into indie writers of the upper midwest you may have heard his name whispered in dark alleys with an equal mix of respect and disdain. His wife thinks he gets carried away at times. He has been featured on television broadcasts, podcasts, and runs a blog for indie authors... but you've still probably never heard of him.

As an avid consumer of comic books, movies, cartoons, and books (especially sci-fi and fantasy) this child of the 80s basically lived out Stranger Things, but shadowy government agencies won't let him say any more than that. He lives in rural Minnesota with his family where he drinks unsafe amounts of coffee; the caffeine shakes keeps the cold from killing them. In his off-time he plays haunted bagpipes in places of low repute, but that's a story for another time.

You can read more of his stuff, find his mailing list, and more books at *www.authorchristopherdschmitz.com*

About
The Maze Runner

The Maze Runner series is a popular dystopian YA science fiction by James Dashner. Over five books (a trilogy, which was also produced as a series of movies, plus two prequel books,) we follow a group of amnesiac teenagers who arrive at a glade in the center of a labyrinth. The passages constantly shift into new alignments and is filled with murderous monsters called Grievers.

Outside the maze lies a world gone mad. Not only is the planet despoiled by solar flares, but also disease. At least some of the teens inside the glade are immune to the Flare (the sickness ravaging the populace.) The teenagers must escape the trials, overcome many enemies who want to use or manipulate them (or kill them outright), and save the ones they care about.

Some of them might be traitors. Some might change their hearts. Some could be infected. Can a group of teenagers on a mission save a world that hates them?

Audacious (Part 1)

Audacious. Acting before anyone asks. Audacity has recently come to my attention as one crucial characteristic which heroes maintain. Audacity decides to do the thing. Audacity reacts. Audacity moves and breathes and shakes and delivers. Audacity can lead to trouble, but it also leads to solutions. In the show, "Gilmore Girls," the grandmother character, Emily Gilmore, contains a remarkable amount of audacity. As her daughter and granddaughter, Lorelai and Rory, rush in to a new private school on Rory's first day, the headmaster greets them in his office, where Emily calmly and demurely stands in her smart pantsuit with a warm cup of coffee in hand. She's already there. Nobody invited her, nobody asked her to participate, yet there she was, prompt, quaffed, and prepared. Throughout the series she displays many examples of audacity, some of which prove detrimental for her relationships, but in general if there's one quality that I admire from Emily Gilmore, it's her audacity. She acts regardless of the consequences. She trusts her gut.

In the book series, "Maze Runner," hero and protagonist Thomas illustrates multiple examples of audacity. He awakes as if in a dream, in a creaky, dark elevator, he knows nothing but his name, and yet his character remains. Within days of arriving in a foreign land knowing no history and no consequences, he leaps into the Maze to help his new-found comrades Minho and Alby as they struggle to return home. From recently arriving in the Glade, the biggest rules he has learned is that the Maze is dangerous and Gladers must stay inside the Glade, especially once the Maze doors close them into the Glade every night. Thomas sees Alby injured in the Maze, and that the doors have begun to shut, and in a heartbeat, Thomas darts into the Maze. He was told to stay. He acted anyway.

When Thomas had arrived in the Glade, he felt the draw of the Maze's power. The boys who were allowed to enter The Maze were called Runners. "He wanted to be a Runner. He *would* be a Runner. Deep inside he knew he had to go out there, into the Maze. Despite everything he'd learned and witnessed firsthand, it called to him as much as hunger or thirst" (pg. 46). Thomas had been told the Maze held danger and destruction, and only death; but as the walls closed in, he could not let danger limit his conviction.

Audacity says, "this will be uncomfortable, but we will deal with that when we get there." Audacity relies on faith – faith in self, faith in hope, and faith in Something Bigger. Thomas knew he was missing answers to the holes in his memory, and he followed that thirst toward the watering hole. And he didn't just jauntily stride toward the Maze, he sprinted with everything within him. He knew he needed to be in the Maze. He knew he needed to help. Come machine or mankind, he trusted that he was part of Something Bigger. He trusted himself enough to handle the danger more than he trusted the safety of the known. What is known is not truly safe; it's just predictable for the short-term. Deep down, Thomas felt that the Glade was temporary, and he was wise to trust that instinct.

So how do we trust enough to advance toward the unknown? How do we trust audacity and self and the unknown, when we stand upon the lush green verdance of our own Glades?

Sprinting into the Maze, starting that journey, serves as one of the hardest steps along the journey. But if you follow the book world, or any story plot, then you'll notice that the steps are challenging all along the way, so the hero expects trials rather than comfort. Life would be much less interesting without obstacles, and humans know that deep down, which is why we seek the adrenaline rush of conflict.

How does the hero then know when to act?

What would happen if the hero did *not* act?

What would happen if all the bad and terrible things *did* happen? What if the worst results became reality?

You, my reader friend, are a hero. You're the protagonist in your story.

Therefore, you need to learn how to trust yourself.

What will happen if you do not?

Thinking through the worst possible outcomes of a scenario can offer some help – because usually, even if the worst outcome happens, that protagonist will see that everything is okay. You're going to be okay. Thomas rushed out into the deadly Maze – he could have immediately died, he could have been punished terribly, he could have lost the little he did have – but he survived, he made some friends, and he proved himself to the Gladers. He proved to himself that he was more capable than he believed.

1) Trust yourself.

You are more capable than you know. You are stronger than you know. You are a being created with unique fingerprints, characteristics, gifts, passions, ideas, and thoughts. You have been entrusted with certain people and obstacles to overcome. There has never been anyone like you and there never will be anyone just like you in the history of mankind. So start to trust that those pieces of your personality are what make you capable.

Start practicing the things which scare you and prove to your brain that you are okay. Your brain will learn from your actions, so begin teaching it to react how you want to react. Do you want to be strong, reliable, courageous, valiant? Do you want to be audacious? Do you want to have a beautiful story? Then accept those challenges which have been created just for you and address them head on. *"For God has not given us a spirit of timidity, but of power, of love, and a sound mind" (2 Timothy 1:7).*

Wisdom is the combination of knowledge plus experience. Wisdom uses what has been gained in order to push onward when necessary. Sometimes you need to wait; sometimes you need to act. And audacity reminds you that you got this.

Paul wrote in 2 Corinthians, *"A thorn in the flesh was given to me, to torment me so I would not exalt myself. Concerning this, I pleaded with the Lord three times to take it away from me. But He said to me, 'My grace is sufficient for you, for power is perfected in weakness.' Therefore, I will most gladly boast all the more about my weaknesses, so that Christ's power may reside in me. So I take pleasure in weaknesses, insults, catastrophes, persecutions, and in pressures, because of Christ. For when I am weak, then I am strong" (12:7-10).*

Even when you feel like you have flaws or need to have a warning label posted across your chest, you have been pieced together with a unique fingerprint and blueprint. Your weakness makes you strong. God works for good for those who trust him.

***

Practical Application

1. What are three characteristics of your personality that you like?

2. Which of these Bible verses spoke you to most? What did the verse reveal to you?

3. What is one weakness that this Bible verse speaks to, and do you see this weakness in yourself?

4. How can you address this weakness or another weakness that you struggle with? What is one thing you can do today to exercise it and make it a strength?

Audacious (Part 2)

"Success is the child of audacity" (Benjamin Disraeli). Being audacious requires self-confidence, trust in Something Bigger, and recognizing that change inevitably happens. You can either let things change you or you can choose what to change. You can let life happen to you or you can happen to life (Jade Teta). Earlier, we focused on how the Maker of the Universe created you piece by piece and entrusted work and people into your life. Today we move onward and outward.

1) Trust Something Bigger.
   "I'm going fishing," Simon Peter said to the disciples.

   "We're coming with you," they told him. They went out and got into the boat, but that night they caught nothing.

   When daybreak came, Jesus stood on the shore. However, the disciples did not know it was Jesus. "Men," Jesus called to them, "you don't have any fish, do you?"

   "No," they answered.

   "Cast the net on the right side of the boat," He told them, "and you'll find some."

   So they did, and they were unable to haul it in because of the large number of fish.

   The disciple, the one Jesus loved, said to Peter, "It is the Lord!"
   (John 21:3-6)

As a friend of mine pointed out about this scenario, "These men were professional fishermen. After Jesus died, they didn't know what to do, so they went back to what they knew: fishing. And they didn't catch a single fish. Can you imagine how tired they were? Can you imagine how hard they had been working, and how frustrated? Or were they even working hard at all, since they hadn't caught anything?"

We don't know how hard they were working, but you can't judge a fisherman by how many fish he's caught. Especially if Jesus wants to make an example out of him. Especially when Jesus needs him to learn a lesson. These friends of Jesus needed to see more of His provision, his presence, and to realize their calling. They'd been following Jesus, but when he died, they didn't know what to do. They knew he'd risen again…but did they know what to do with that? I guess not. They went back to fishing. They went to the work they knew. They got in the boat.

The twelve disciples of Jesus had different lives after he came and left. Judas was out of the picture at this point. Seven of them worked in that boat. Where did the other four go?

The hero plotline requires hard work. The hero plotline will at times require the protagonist to work all night, to continue throwing the nets, to stay in the boat. Sometimes the protagonist must leave the boat. Sometimes the protagonist must cast the net in a new direction.

Maybe you've been working, busting it, and are tired. Maybe you're worn out and weary. Take heart. Jesus is there. Maybe you're sitting on the sidelines, withdrawn among the crowd, shivering under a blanket, terrified. Don't be one of the four missing the meeting. Come on. Jesus awaits. He's got this great job for you to do. He will bring the strength to accomplish it.

Being unsure of the next step doesn't mean you stop in your tracks. Jesus is walking on the beach, waiting for just the right time, to cook you a fish breakfast. Yum-o! Maybe those disciples needed a night in the boat, busting it, to appreciate the light streaming across Jesus' face. They needed the empty nets to appreciate how many fish he brought to them. They needed to wait on Jesus to understand *He* was providing their fish, their fulfillment, their fruition. At just the right time.

2) This is all temporary anyway.

"Minho grunted. 'Being careful hasn't gotten us squat. It's all or nothing now, baby'" (pg. 281).

Drawing to the climax of the book, Thomas and his Glader friends decide to act as a group. Thomas' audacity served his peers and reminded them of the bigger picture: they'd been careful and reliable since landing in The Glade. And being careful had served them for a while, but the times had changed. This beautiful world continues to revolve, and you will never be where you are in this place in the universe again. Change intertwines within the sun's rising and setting. Even when the known may seem constant and stable, change awaits. Adventure awaits. These dazzling moments which may seem safe and constant will change at some point, so practice who you want to be when adventure comes knocking.

I am someone who likes my schedule. I like knowing where I can insert time to eat, to exercise, to watch endless episodes of Gilmore Girls on Netflix, and to get my work done. I like predictability. There is a time for predictability, but too much control and too much predictability also create boredom. The perfect mixture of control and chaos creates balance. There will always be events which occur to create chaos. And there will be events which you can control. (Although you always get to choose how you act and how you react.) "Trust is the opposite of control" (Jill Coleman). Whatever season you find yourself in right now, a season of chaos, a season of control, a season of change, you can trust--what was that? Oh yeah--you can trust yourself and Something (or Someone) Bigger.

Now remember this, practice, sharpen, and memorize the facts: With faith in your abilities and self, with faith in that Bigger reality which has entrusted this moment to you, you can overcome. You are the hero. It's all or nothing now, baby.

***

Practical Application

1. Are you riding the Struggle Boat? Where do you feel like you apply in this story – have you been casting the nets all night? Are you sleeping on the boat? Or are you given up on the boat and gone back to land?

2. Name one time you have seen God acting to help you make headway in a struggle.

3. List the expectations you had which are contributing to your "Struggle Boat." What is the struggle? What were you expecting that did not happen?

4. Do you think you need to keep working, to keep waiting, or to move on?

5. What one action can you take that shows you trust yourself, God, and that you can endure this season?

Everybody Needs a Chuck

What's the difference between humility and self-deprecation? Can an audacious someone also be humble? And in the Maze Runner, why did Thomas care so much about Chuck?

Think of the famous warriors we study from the stories of old – the legends, the rulers, the patriots, the freedom fighters – and what picture do you draw? What adjectives would you provide to describe them? Bold. Fierce. Strong. Valiant. Brave. Would you ever say, "humble"? Would that be a first-word choice?

Humility has four definitions:
1. Not proud or arrogant; modest
2. Having a feeling of insignificance or inferiority
3. Low in rank, importance, status, quality; lowly
4. Courteously respectful

Humility shows up all over the place in the Bible. Deuteronomy 8:2-3 reminds, *"Remember that the Lord your God led you on the entire journey these forty years in the wilderness, so that He might humble you and test you to know what was in your heart, whether or not you would keep His commands. He humbled you by letting you go hungry; then He gave you manna to eat, which you and your fathers had not known, so that you might learn that man does not live on bread alone but on every word that comes from the mouth of the Lord."*

We find our true selves in times of trouble. God provides these opportunities to let us see who we are and who we can be. He also allows us to see his provision as our Shepherd. He allows us to see what we can be and *whose* we are. He loves us enough to allow us to become stronger; and remember he's there with us the entire time. This builds our reliance on him, teaching us those hard-learned, hard-earned lessons of trust, faith, and humility.

The Jews for Jesus website offered a unique take on the idea of humility. "In the Bible, the most common word group displaying the meaning of humble uses the related words 'ani' and 'anav'. 'Ani' usually denotes a condition of circumstance. Those who are 'ani' are suffering or afflicted and as a result find themselves in a lowly condition, whether physically, materially or socially. This affliction is often imposed by someone else: usually, the wicked...There is a related verb, 'anah' (to "humble") that not only refers to what one might do to one's enemies but also to what one does to oneself as a spiritual practice or what God uses to bring about repentance (Deuteronomy 8:2-3)... Often, being an 'ani' in circumstance leads to being an 'anav' in character...The difference between the two is that the 'ani' is needy and must depend on God to meet his or her needs; the 'anav' is humble because he or she has chosen to depend on God. The first is circumstantial; the second is a mark of character." (Rich Robinson)

***

Part of the plot of Maze Runner was that the boys in the Glade were gifted, and placed intentionally within the program to see which of their attributes would be the perfect, precise mix of abilities to survive despite the worst odds. The boys' memories were wiped, and they were planted with specific drops of memories to attend the Glade with them, along with new names. The names were given based on historical people of influence.

"So...Thomas," [Chuck] said through a huge bite of mashed potatoes. "Who am I nicknamed after?"

Thomas couldn't help shaking his head--here they were, about to embark on probably the most dangerous task of their lives, and Chuck was curious where he'd gotten his nickname. "I don't know, Darwin, maybe? The dude who figured out evolution."

"I bet no one's ever called him a dude before." Chuck took another big bite, and seemed to think that was the best time to talk, full mouth and all. "You know, I'm really not all that scared...I mean, last few nights, sitting in the Homestead, just waiting for a Griever to come in and steal one of us was the worst thing I've ever done. At least now we're taking it to them, trying something..." (324).

Chuck was not well-liked among the Gladers. He was not on the council, he was not a leader, he did not draw the crowds in with his star personality and ruggedly handsome good looks. Chuck did not seem to belong in The Glade. Newt adapted well, ready to try ideas, a friend to the willing, and courageous in his tasks. Minho followed orders, used his strength and perseverance to run his course, and obviously had a memory of stone, capable of learning and memorizing in a snap. Thomas had his audacity, his willingness to run farther and faster, and his loyalty. And Chuck? Chuck was a bit clumsy, a bit annoying, and scared. He wasn't quick. He wasn't quick-witted. He waited for instructions. He lacked leadership capability. He lacked skill; he picked up the trash.

But Chuck was Thomas' friend when everyone else looked away.

Chuck believed in Thomas from the start.

Chuck believed life could and would be better.

Chuck gave Thomas a reason to want to survive. Chuck inspired Thomas to take the hard steps, because Chuck was worth helping.

Perhaps Chuck's greatest gift was his humility. His meekness. His simplicity. He didn't require perfect people and circumstances; he didn't demand more from others; he didn't seize attention and commodities. He did his job. He stayed the course. He took courage when necessary.

"Chuck's pudgy face was there, staring with frightened eyes. But then they lit up and a smile spread across his face. Despite it all, despite the terrible crappiness of it all, Chuck smiled" (298).

So you see, we all need a Chuck. We need a friend who can smile even during the grievances. When the grief comes, where's your Chuck? Are you Chuck?

Let's go back to those four definitions of humility:

1. Modest
2. Awareness of smallness
3. Awareness of rank
4. Courteously respectful

Humility is not simply lacking in pride; humility is not simply thinking less of self. Humility has many layers. Humility has a lot of intention. Modesty protects; smallness realizes bigness of others; rank recognizes there are those above and those below; and courteous respect treats all with dignity. Humility serves the leader in his power so that he sees the significance of each member of his tribe. Humility serves the follower in that he knows his worth.

Charles Darwin was known as a leader in the scientific community of his day; he was the man who made popular the idea of, "survival of the fittest." The Creators of the Maze must have seen in Chuck the necessary characteristics to inspire warfare and survival. They understood what made humans motivated the most: life and love. They saw in Chuck this ability to befriend and build up, a scarce commodity in times of trouble.

In these days where almost everyone has a platform and the opportunity to make a staunch position, sometimes the best is the calm, quiet one. Being willing to accept that every leader follows another reminds even the smallest of us that the quiet smile serves as inspiration for even the most courageous of hearts. We all need a Chuck at our side in the halls of the maze. We all need a Chuck to follow along. We all need a Chuck to inspire us to lead.

Even if you're the Thomas, or the Newt, the Minho, Teresa, or even the Gally…everybody can be a Chuck. He's a gift. A rather scarce commodity. And one of the most valuable of them all.

Practical Application

1. Who do you see yourself leading? List their names:

2. Who do you trust as an authority figure/example for life:

3. Are you wandering in some kind of personal 'desert'? What's the heart issue in play?

4. What can you do to take one step forward in faith through that desert?

5. List one characteristic you have that will allow you take this step forward, or one character trait you can improve in order to accomplish this step:

6. Do you see yourself as an "ani" or an "anav"? How does this influence your decisions? What does it mean about your character?

Into The Trials

"I'm assuming you've figured this out by now, but many of the things that happen to you are solely for the purpose of judging and analyzing your responses. And yet it's not really an experiment as much as it is…constructing a blueprint. …These situations inflicted upon you are called the Variables, and each one has been meticulously thought out. And though I can't tell you everything at this time, it's vital that you know this much: these trials you're going through are for a very important cause. Continue to respond well to the Variables, continue to survive, and you'll be rewarded with the knowledge that you've played a part in saving the human race. And yourselves, of course." (The Scorch Trials, pg. 55)

The first hard step requires leaving the Glade. To step beyond comfort, to step outside the borders you've allowed yourself to set for safety, goes against human nature. Human nature intrinsically clings to safety and the familiar known. The typical human will choose dissatisfied comfort over fulfilled discomfort. It is only the rarer individual who leaves the Glade and runs into the Maze.

The maze is full of danger. The maze is full of unknown twists, turns, dead ends, and frustration. The maze offers no comfort with its sterile, cement walls and limited shelter. The maze is, however, the opportunity.

I attended a training weekend for LesMills BodyFlow™, to be certified to teach the hour-long Tai Chi, Pilates, and Yoga program. To drive the four hours, rent the hotel room by myself, and walk into an unfamiliar gym with unfamiliar faces was so overwhelming for my introverted self to handle. The training began and hours into the work, my inner voice yelled, "Run for your life!" I had serious fight or flight reactions. The uber-fit trainer stood at the front of the group, providing a professional and amazing educational experience, while I shrank into the back of the room, doubting that I belonged. I was one of the bigger females in that room. I had never instructed a fitness class in a professional setting. I did not feel qualified, capable, or confident. The instructor told us to get into groups and practice presenting our tracks. I led my track, the warm-up. The girl next to me pressed, "Play" on her phone to begin the music. She got the first cue. She missed the second. Then she crumpled. Her doubt won. It didn't matter that we were all there, feeling that exact same way. She left. I'd wanted to flee, too. But even more than that, I didn't want to be the girl who left.

You can always run away. Failure is always an option. Giving up is somehow second nature, the natural reaction.

But failure is your opportunity to learn, to start over, to find out how to improve.

Be the one who stays.

"Frypan pushed. 'Well, what makes him any more in charge than this whispering dude? How're we supposed to know who to listen to and who to ignore?' Thomas knew it was a good question, but going back just didn't feel right. 'The voice is just a test, I bet. We need to keep going'" (The Scorch Trials, pg. 77).

Those inner doubts will be loud and proud, offering more reasons to run away than to keep going. The Gladers left the Maze only to find themselves in further trials, where scorch and lightning and thirst threatened their lives. But they had been told specifically to travel one hundred miles, journey through the trials, and get to the Safe Haven. They knew the reward. They were provided a specific goal to accomplish. They knew they could not, should not turn back. Most did not make it to the Safe Haven.

But.

"We don't quit when we are doing God's work" (Charlotte Richards).

We humans don't always recognize the fact that we've been given specific tasks to accomplish. Sometimes it seems like we are just here, alone, hoping for some pizza. But each beautiful soul brought to this planet has a purpose, in fact several purposes, and tools, to add to the mix of the human story. *"For God has not given us a spirit of timidity, but of power, love, and a sound mind" (2 Timothy 1:7).* God built each human with individual capabilities, courage, and charisma to accomplish specific tasks, journey through individualized tests, and to contribute to the woven tapestry of interactions. The people you meet need you in some way, and you need them. You offer your people something different than I do. You communicate to your community differently than I do. And that's a beautiful product.

One challenging lesson to grasp is that the conflict serves you. Your Trials serve you. Your Maze serves you. They offer you the opportunity to see who you are, whose you are, and who you can be. Would you rather be bored in Happy Land where everything is easy and the cotton candy clouds continually float by? Or would you improve, triumph, and explore? Would you rather take the challenging path and find out that you can be so much more than you ever imagined? Would you rather endure the test of faith, or stay safe in your unhappiness? Because we are not truly happy inside of our comfort zone. Yes, comfortable, but often dissatisfied. Be uncomfortable and create bliss. You don't know how much you can do until you test yourself to find out.

"Well if it were easy it wouldn't be much of a test." (Amenadiel the Angel[2])

People complain, "Why does God let bad things happen?" Well, the answer has many layers, but consider this as one of them: God wants you to know who you are, whose you are, and who you can be. If the test were easy, if everything were easy, then we'd all be bored and sad. You have been granted a life greater. You are capable of so much more than you realize. I promise.

"Make your own attitude that of Christ Jesus, who, existing in the form of God, did not consider equality with God as something to be used for His own advantage. Instead He emptied

---

[2] A fictional character from comic books and the television show *Lucifer*

Himself by assuming the form of a slave, taking on the likeness of men. And when He had come as a man in His external form, He humbled Himself by becoming obedient to the point of death--even to death on a cross" (Philippians 2:5-8).

Jesus serves as our ultimate hero example. He came to earth, showed us how to be a hero, and gave us the wisdom we need to continue sharing light and life. He responded with kindness, valor, and strength. He was taken by authorities, slapped across the face, beaten with a whip, the ends cast of bone, and scraps of pottery which tore the skin from his back; his clothes were yanked from him; soldiers shoved thorns into his skull in the shape of a crown, then spit upon him. And he was rejected, betrayed, alone, humiliated, torn, scorned. Crowds, thousands of people, shouted for his head. Nails surged through his wrists as authorities forced a heavy, splintered, wooden beam onto his shredded, bloody back. He did not speak a word to them in anger. He did not run away. He did not shout in outrage or call down fire. He stumbled up that dusty hill, then slowly suffocated upon a cross. Our provider. Our great rescuer. Our God with us. Our ultimate hero and example.

He had spoken to his disciples, his best friends, explaining to them in words they couldn't comprehend that he would be broken and bruised, and that he loved them ever so dearly that he was willing to lead by example. He would not back down. Instead he said, "Do this in remembrance of me." So many of us participate in the pittance of Communion, a sip of juice and a bit of cracker, and bow our heads in prayer. We say this is how we connect with our Creator.

Perhaps consider that as he took on that burden, he committed to showing us the purest form of faith, to DO this in remembrance of Him. Be broken. Be brave. Be courageous. Act in the name of love. Act in kindness, generosity, without judgment. He who planted the first seeds of trees and sewed together the wings of hummingbirds and butterflies and eagles, who sprinkled the seas with salt and slathered snow upon the highest mountain peaks, he who took the form of human and trudged the dust, understands the gloom of that which makes your heart shudder. What are you afraid of? Can you meet it, head on, in remembrance of Him? Can you raise a glass and courageously accept the cup which you have been dealt?

The test will not be easy. The task will not appear light. But your crucible calls to you by name, and the Prince of Peace stands by your side. He conquered death. He has won the battle. This trepidation you sense? It's your battle cry.

"Haven't I commanded you: 'be strong and courageous'? Do not be afraid or discouraged, for the Lord your God is with you wherever you go" (Joshua 1:9).

Do that thing which scares you the most. Pursue peace by taking on the task which calls your heart. Your great rescuer walks by your side, going before and behind, knowing full well the pain, the loss, the crushing heartache, the burning rejection, the dark loneliness. He conquered it, he rose, he returned, and he will pass within your marrow through the scorch. You are now the protagonist, the hero, His boots on the ground. Time to leave the Maze.

***

Practical Application:

1. Who are you when the lights go out? Name one conflict you recently experienced and write out objectively how you handled it.

2. What can you do better if this happens again?

3. What three activities bring you joy? Why do you want to do these tasks?

4. Do you want this because it was taught to you or because your soul needs it?

5. What are three phrases or events which enrage /frighten you?

6. Do these make you feel this way because it was taught to you or because you have a better solution?

7. What is a better solution?

8. Is this solution best for the people involved or for you?

9. Can you do the solution in an attitude of love and service? How?

10. How does implementing this solution impact your life in ten years?

11. What three steps can you take to implement the solution in combination with the three activities which bring you joy?

12. What happens if you do not do this?

Tools for the MAZE

"At dinner Minho had told [Thomas] an old story--one of the bizarre and random things he remembered from before--about a woman trapped in a maze. She escaped by never taking her right hand off the walls of the maze, sliding it along as she walked. In doing so, she was forced to turn right at every turn, and the simple laws of physics and geometry ensured that eventually she found the exit. It made sense" (Maze Runner, pg. 200)

Mathematically, a typical maze with an entrance on one side and an exit on the other can be solved using this type of method. Keep one hand on one wall and walk. If the maze has an exit in the middle, is an infinite maze, or has moving walls, this method may not work. Upon researching further into this concept, one website I found stated that this rule may also not work if the maze has portals, no exit, or is a dead pigeon. I hope your life, your maze, is not a dead pigeon. May the odds be ever in your favor in that case.

In a way, friend, life is a maze. We are on this beautiful, thought-provoking, riddle of a journey. There are unknowns, there are dead ends, and there are new paths to course. There will one day be an end, but the adventure lies within the discovery of the path along the way. As Rebecca Solnit wrote in, "Wanderlust," "That (labyrinth)...became a world whose rules I lived by, and I understood the moral of mazes: sometimes you have to turn your back on your goal to get there, sometimes you're farthest away when you're closest, sometimes the only way is the long one. After that careful walking and looking down, the stillness was deeply moving...It was breathtaking to realize that in the labyrinth, metaphors and meanings could be conveyed spatially. That when you seem farthest from your destination is when you suddenly arrive is a very pat truth in words, but a profound one to find with your feet."

Am I then saying there's just this endless riddle? Nah. Am I saying there's endless possibilities? Yes. There are constant possibilities to learn, to run, to explore, to rise to challenge, to climb, and to meet God within the tasks he entrusts to you. My daughter asked me the other day about the size of her legs, and if they were too big. I looked down at her nine-year old beautiful ballerina self and I reminded her of the ultimate truth: God made her piece by piece with the muscles and mind and heart that she needed to do the good work he has prepared for her to do. And you know when things click? They click when you're teaching others. They click when you're in the grind and getting those hands dirty. That is what I have found, anyway. I told her there are four key elements all humans require for living the best life.

The M.A.Z.E. is the answer.

Meditate. Know God; draw near to his heart. Study the Bible, the fresh and living, active words of God conveyed to us. Pray constantly. Seek God's wisdom. Meditate upon his power dwelling within your spirit and blood.

Act. Take action. Walk an hour every day. Keep moving. Lift heavy weights, breathe deeply, and do the work presented upon your heart. Thomas knew within his marrow he needed to be a runner. He didn't know why, but he knew it. What good work presses upon your spirit? What do you need to do to help others and to serve? What do you need to do to bring light and life to your world?

Zen. Let's be honest, not a lot of words begin with Z, and although the origination of the word, "zen," has Buddhist origins, it has come into urban life meaning to be calm, to be quiet, to practice peace. Maybe interpret it as, 'zone out'? Create time in your day to relax and intentionally let go of stress. Unclench those fists. Curl your toes in the soft grass. Embrace the senses – breathe deeply, touch the softness of skin and flowers and the grittiness of dirt; taste the sweetness of berries; awe within the colors of the sunset; dance along to the song of the stars. Let go of worry and instead recognize God's abundance. Spend time daily practicing peace.

Eat. Get that belly full and eat lean proteins, and lots of fibrous vegetables and fruit. Drink lots of fresh water. Eat before you get hungry, and do not eat so much that you are cram-packed full. Fuel your life with goodness and taste those wonderful flavors which offer you energy to endure this journey.

MAZE living.

Four simple tools. One thrilling adventure.

Keep your hand on the wall, our great Provider, Shepherd, guide and guard, who reigns as the Prince of Peace, the King of Kings, the mettle in your blood, the iron in your armor, the guardian of your spirit. Love the Lord your God with all your courage. Love the Lord your God with all your energy. Love the Lord your God through your talents. Love the Lord your God through your skills and abilities, through the strength in your hands.

What's that sound? Do you hear the battle drums?
Meditate. Act. Zen. Eat.
Get ready, runner. Do you hear the war cry?
"You hem me in behind and before,
and you lay your hand upon me.
Such knowledge is too wonderful for me,
too lofty for me to attain.

Where can I go from your Spirit?
Where can I flee from your presence?
If I go up to the heavens, you are there;
if I make my bed in the depths, you are there.
If I rise on the wings of the dawn,
if I settle on the far side of the sea,
even there your hand will guide me,

your right hand will hold me fast.
If I say, "Surely the darkness will hide me
and the light become night around me,"
even the darkness will not be dark to you;
the night will shine like the day,
for darkness is as light to you.

For you created my inmost being;
you knit me together in my mother's womb.
I praise you because I am fearfully and wonderfully made;
your works are wonderful,
I know that full well.
My frame was not hidden from you
when I was made in the secret place,
when I was woven together in the depths of the earth.
Your eyes saw my unformed body;
all the days ordained for me were written in your book
before one of them came to be...

Search me, God, and know my heart;
test me and know my anxious thoughts.
See if there is any offensive way in me,
and lead me in the way everlasting."

Psalm 139:5-17, 23-24

Your maker, your maze-builder, your earth-Creator, your universe collector, stands before, behind, around, and within your powerful spirit. You are flesh and blood built for these tasks which weigh upon your heart. You have been presented with challenge, with awe, with trepidation, and this is the battle cry calling you away from comfort and into courage. You have been called forth; you have been redeemed for times as these. Your good works yearn to be accomplished. The test is the path forward. The walls stand sturdy. Keep your hand on the wall.

The battle drums grow louder, more intense. Your heart writhes within your chest. Even your blood pulses to the rhythm of a life greater. The doors are closing. Your friends are out there, they need your help. They stumble and fall, Glader. Your life, your freedom, your bliss, they're outside those doors.

Three seconds…

Two…

Run.

***

Practical Application:

1. Thomas recognized he needed to be a Runner. What one action do I need to take that I have been putting off?

2. What portion of the verses from Psalm 139 apply to me in doing this action?

3. Am I afraid of doing this work? Am I overwhelmed by doing something new, am I unsure of my skills to do it, or am I waiting on someone else to do it for me?

4. What is one activity which relaxes me? Challenge yourself to do it for thirty minutes today.

Author Bio - Kadee Carder

Fierce yet sparkly, she rallies seekers to thrive in their stories. The goal is magic, the medium is ink, and the fuel is coffee. And sometimes pizza. She teaches English on the university level when she's not dancing around the living room with her family, lifting heavy at the gym, traveling the planet, or binging superhero shows.

INSURRECTION, INCOMPLETE, INDELIBLE, HERE BE DRAGONS, EARTHSHINE and non-fiction inspirational KINGDOM COME roll out perilous motives, twisty plots, and daring protagonists. Grab some real estate and your copy of her latest adventure and follow along on KadeeCarder.com.

Facebook: *https://www.facebook.com/kadeecarderink*
Instagram: @kadeecarderink

About Insurrection

The last thing Saylor MacTavish remembers is a cry for help. Now she's fighting for her life. Deep within a mysterious island, strange creatures rule and an army of fire reigns.

Banding together with her closest friends, Saylor's story twists through dark secrets, high-tech weaponry, and ultimately faces an enemy bigger than herself. Will she find the strength to overcome her past or will she discover the power to be the hero the world needs?

INSURRECTION, INCOMPLETE, INDELIBLE, HERE BE DRAGONS, and EARTHSHINE follow the McConnell clan and Alliance Military Guard, a series for the seeker of YA Sci-Fi Action Adventures.

Insurrection

Life requires moxie. Yes? Spunk? Life takes a little fight, doesn't it? A little fight to laugh at the chaos, a little fight not to yell, a little fight to get out of bed at 3:00 AM when the baby wakes, and a little fight every night to put away the latest novel and go to bed and start all over.

Life takes a lot of love, too. Love instigates a lot of the fight within me, as a mom. I began working on the INSURRECTION trilogy while earning my Master of Fine Arts degree in Creative Writing, pregnant, working full-time as an office manager of a church. At that point in my life I began to understand the depths of what it takes to chase after dreams and shake up the stars. In the years since beginning this journey with Saylor, I've sat for hours hunkered over my laptop, chatted with hundreds of people, and even flown across the country to meet with publishers in order to make this adventure more than just a fun story I shared with my own girlfriends as we played in our backyards twenty years ago. When Saylor first appeared as a character to me, she was a boy, because when I played in my backyard, only boys had adventures. It's time to change that, friends, because girls can rock a baseball bat, obstacle course, and beachside kiss just as good as the best of them.

We humans have to be stronger than we ever imagine, love ourselves in the process, and dig in when the ground seems to sink. We not only relish adventures, we create them.

That's the basis of Saylor's story in my young adult science fiction trilogy, INSURRECTION:

The last thing Saylor McTavish remembers is a cry for help. Now she's fighting for her life. Deep within a mysterious island, strange things are happening and an army of fire reigns.

Banding together with her closest friends, she escaped abuse at the Oak Point Girl's Home and fled across the high seas, only to end up a prisoner again, this time at the mercy of the Alliance Military Guard. They are at war, and now so is she.

Follow Saylor as she unlocks the dark secrets of the island, learns to wield high-tech weaponry, and ultimately faces an enemy bigger than herself. Will she find the strength to overcome her past or will she discover the power to be the hero the world needs?

***

My parents encouraged me to try a myriad assortment of activities when I was younger. Softball stuck. I played the sport for over ten years, loving almost every minute. In my last season where we didn't win a single game, that was harsh, but hey, I learned I loved the sport no matter what. In order to help me improve, my dad drilled a hole in a softball and strung it up on this horizontal branch on a large tree in our backyard. I'd spend hours slamming that softball up and around the branch, perfecting my swing. Being an overly-creative, left-handed child, I'd invent all sorts of scenarios in which I'd have to hit something over and over and over....and just think, if a softball could fly on its own, and was ON FIRE, what would YOU do?! And the basic premise for Insurrection wiggled its way into my imagination. I presented the idea to my three friends, who'd play imaginary games with me at recess, and suddenly the four of us became fearless fighters, saving the world from flying fireballs. With my husband's help, I've updated the idea to call them Oxinals, and they are autonomous, artificially intelligent sentinels, which can kill any living creature with one single touch. We'd need some brave warriors to save us, yes?

You may never have to battle autonomous, artificially intelligent sentinels, but you will have the opportunity to face your own dragons. You will receive the opportunity to make crucial decisions and step into your own amazing hero plotline. Saylor started off as a lonely, frustrated, unsure girl, who stole a boat, ran away, and disaster followed. But then she found passion and purpose in the center of the thing that scared her most. Maybe you're dreaming of big things and great stories. Maybe you're stuck facing overwhelming odds, and fears which leave you crippled. Or maybe, just maybe, it's time to run toward some fire.

"Let me experience Your faithful love in the morning, for I trust in You. Reveal to me the way I should go because I long for You" (Psalm 143:8). David sought confirmation that he'd be alright. He wanted a guarantee he would do The Right Thing. The thing is, God constantly provided refuge for David. God brought him out of danger, even though David felt the weight of shadows and their mystery. But he also lived in the days before Jesus came and rocked death's world. Hebrews gives us this promise: *"God Himself has said, "I will never leave you or forsake you.' Therefore, we may boldly say: The Lord is my helper; I will not be afraid. What can man do to me?" (Hebrews 6-13:5 HCSB)*

Wherever you boldly go in this universe, God will go with you. You are completed by God's presence. He's that unwavering yoke. With faith in him, where do you end, and where does God begin?

With God in me, we are limitless.

If what I'm doing brings joy to God, and I am using my gifts for good, then we are limitless. Forget "enough." Go beyond.

Be loving; be wise; be kind.

By doing these things you make The Right Choice. It doesn't matter if others don't understand your motivation or big picture. They have their own business to attend to. You have yours.

The Thing You're Supposed To Do may look different than you thought. Saylor found passion along the way, and it looked completely different than she expected. Don't wait for a sign or a moment of confirmation. If you've got the fear of doing it, that's the thing to do. If you've got the nagging desire burning the back of your brain, that's the path. It's calling you. Go find that fire.

***

Who are you when the lights go out?

How do you react when your patience runs out?

Who do you want to be when the lights go out?

What does *"Let me experience Your faithful love in the morning, for I trust in You. Reveal to me the way I should go because I long for You" (Psalm 143:8)* say to you?

What is the nature of God to you when the lights go out?

God Himself has said, "I will never leave you or forsake you.' Therefore, we may boldly say: The Lord is my helper; I will not be afraid. What can man do to me?" (Hebrews 6-13:5 HCSB)

List three things you can apply to your life from this verse.

Indelible Choices

We want to see heroes who make good decisions. We want heroes who do the good thing, the hard thing, the right thing. Throughout the INSURRECTION series, Saylor panders and falters at times, and even begins to listen to her villainous enemy along the way. Readers say they want Saylor to make better decisions than that! Readers want heroes/protagonists to make the better decision. Readers want to see protagonists DO BETTER THAN. Am I right?

Have you ever danced with the devil in the pale moonlight?

But seriously, have you ever, especially in your teens, made the decision to go against what you knew deep down to be right? Were you ever in a hard position where you didn't know what was right or wrong, so you tried your best, but found yourself in what seemed like the wrong place at the wrong time? Have you ever found yourself listening to the lies of fear, hate, or doubt wandering about your brain?

Well, friends, this is what I want my readers to really ponder.

Sometimes we listen to our demons. Sometimes we listen to our doubts instead of our faith.

Sometimes we listen to the crowd, or the false news, or the scary whispers, instead of finding the truth from the Commander. Sometimes we make the decision to go into the tunnel instead of standing still.

I wanted Saylor to face some hard decisions and waver. I wanted her to have to rally. I wanted to let her take a wild risk that turned out a bit sour. Why? Because I wanted to give her a chance to redeem herself. I wanted to give her Commander a chance to let her know the truth about who she was, who HE was, and all she could do. Saylor needed to see the darkness so she could choose the light. Too many spoilers there? I don't know.

Additionally, I wanted to let readers get to know the villain, Wellington Breame, and judge him for themselves. Was he a big, fat liar? Or was he a pitiable genius? We can't often deal with our enemies until we've met them and named them.

Saylor needed some impossible moments to realize her full power. Could she have done that if she'd "made the right decision"? Sometimes there is no "right" decision. The right decision finds us. The right decision helps you realize your full potential, because it's exactly the decision you needed to make to be better.

***

At that time, Hanani the seer came to King Asa of Judah and said to him, "Because you depended on the king of Aram and have not depended on the Lord your God, the army of the king of Aram has escaped from your hand. Were not the Cushites and Libyans a vast army with many chariots and horsemen? When you depended on Yahweh, He handed them over to you. For the eyes of Yahweh roam throughout the earth to show Himself strong for those whose hearts are completely His.
2 Chronicles 16:7-9a

One decision after another, you earn the opportunity to learn and to remember. You earn the opportunity to employ wisdom. The Bible can often seem like a foreign object, a list of other people's stories in other times. Again and again, God reminds us that he seeks us, that he stays strong, and that he simply wants people in his tribe who seek him in return. He serves as our strength when we have none. He will bring the victory, the redemption, while we seek his heart. The easy thing to do is to say, "Trust God with those decisions." The hard thing to do is to live that out, by choosing the decision which points people to God.

This can be quite challenging, as many of our decisions may not, on the surface level, seem to have anything to do with "God's plan" and what is "best." Do I apply for this job or for this other one? Do I buy this house or this other house? Do I walk down this street or this other one? Should I take my vitamins in the morning or at night? Do I scramble the eggs or fry them?

The eyes of Yahweh roam the earth to show Himself strong for those whose hearts are completely His.

What motivates your decisions? And to whom will you give the glory for the final results? Perhaps the decision is not as important as the journey through it.

Dragons

In all the battles I've seen, in all the training exercises, and the obstacles I've had to climb in my few days on this planet, I'd have to say that day on the beach was one of the most memorable. I hated tugging that ridiculous net along that beach. I felt like I wasn't getting anywhere.

All of my efforts felt pointless and resistant. With each jerk forward, I made almost no progress. Anger gurgled in a knot within my ribs. Norita wrenched ahead of me along that beach. He shouldn't have--he was a weakling who couldn't even keep his lunch down.

I struggled, sweat dripping down the sides of my face, burning into my eyes, and sliming up my hands so they slipped along the rope, seared. Blisters welled up on my palms, and my back broiled with a fervent, charring ache.

"You gotta pull your own weight, Thompson!" Burkman brought me back. He drew up to my side, hands flailing. He seemed to be everywhere.

"You have to get past those demons! You have to fight them; you have to beat them down. Those voices that tell you to stop, those are wrong. Those voices lie. They steal your victory. Out there be dragons, but in here--" He tapped my chest, "--here lodges your sword and shield. You give up, you'll never win. You? Give up? That's not you. You are a victor. You are a success. You have what it takes. Keep going, Thompson. Success isn't a finish line; success isn't one moment that makes you great. Success is tackling those obstacles one at a time. Success is dragging this weight until you aren't supposed to carry it any more. This net is your objective. This finish line, this is where you gotta get. You don't stop until you get that net across the line. You can't stop. You won't stop. You carry that weight. Nobody else can pull it. That's your weight. Now, you don't give up. Look around. We need you to cross this line. I don't care if you do this for us, or for yourself, or if you do this for your mama across the water. Your job, soldier, is to bring this net across this line. You can't win every challenge. Tucker, you have this moment right here to build up to the moments coming to get you. Tomorrow could be harder. That's okay. Because you'll have survived this, right here, right now. Drag that net. Cross the line. The line is all we got."

Through the tumult of his words, I buried myself in the forward movement. Me versus the sand. Me versus the weight. The weight withheld its grace, but I secured that rope within my hands and grasped with all I had. Head down, straining with all the gumption I had within me, I hoisted that bag of dumb weights until I crashed into Steele's chest.

(Excerpt from HERE BE DRAGONS
by Kadee Carder)

***

A man walking through a valley hears a thundering roar. He stops in his tracks. A giant boulder tumbles to the ground before him, blocking his path between the narrow mountain pass. He must get to the village beyond; it's his destination. He cannot turn back; days of travel lay behind him and he has limited supplies.

Does the man yell? Shout? Roar in callous anger at the fallen rock? Would it do any good to yell at the rock? No. He must find a way over the boulder. He takes one step forward, and another, digging his fingers into the crusty earth, plotting footholds up, up, and over that wall. As he jumps down the final steps beyond the boulder, he looks back. His arms tremble with power, he slaps his gritty palms together vigorously. The wind coursing through his lungs inundates his hearty chest. He overcame the rock, and he continues on his way toward home.

Are you battling fallen rocks? Are you stuck? Are you struggling with hard things happening and you don't know what to do about them? Ownership, owning your decisions and experiences in the light of adversity, offers the foothold over the boulder. You cannot control outcomes, others, or the falling rocks. You just have to deal with those falling rocks. Those monsters. Those dragons. Those feelings of inadequacy or unimportance. You can control your decisions and how you act. You can choose to search for footholds rather than yell at the rock. Instead of complaining about the rock, instead of shouting angry words at the shadows, you can instead move forward with gratitude, thankful for the rock and all it teaches you.

See, those monsters, those shadows, those obstacles, they teach you who your soul craves to be. They show you just where you need to go. Did the man need to get home? Yes. But did he need an opportunity to see how strong he could be? Yes, even more, in fact. More than the final destination is the journey along the way. This life you've got, it's pretty brilliant. It's filled with moments where you can choose to be the hero. When you embrace the challenge, when you act with purpose, when you stay the course, that's when you fully realize life itself. "Everything you have ever wanted is sitting on the other side of fear" (George Addair). In facing your fears, you shine the light on the shadows of what you truly need to do on this planet.

I found this myself after receiving a horrible review on one of my books. If you have ever made anything, you understand the risks involved of letting all your inside hopes and dreams be smashed to bits by an unhappy audience. Well. I've always been competitive and a high achiever. I go big. I do my best. It's all on the line. Also, if you've ever created anything, you know that your first attempt at something isn't what you will eventually be able to do. I wrote a trilogy of young adult novels and I love them with all I have. I did my best. Apparently, not everyone agrees. That's okay. That's life, folks. That's art. Well. As I read this horrible review, and allthefeelings overcame me, my husband straight up said, "If you can't take the bad reviews, then you might as well give up now." I took a long walk that night under the starry sky.

First of all, even though my heart sank, my feet didn't. My heart didn't stop beating. In fact, the next morning, waking up to the cleared out cobwebs of loss and horror, and realizing everything I believed about myself had changed....I found a blissful freedom. As if the shades had lifted. As if the sun shone, no matter what. See, the Son does shine no matter what. I've been put on this planet for a reason. I'm not always sure what it is, but he gave me these stories to share to encourage people. He gave me stories so I can learn to tell better stories. If that means taking some hard hits, then bring them on. I took an objective look at my writing, at my weaknesses where I could improve, at my strengths, and where I needed to dig in and sharpen the tools and my ability to use them. Meeting failure head-on made me reach higher. Every hero faces that in his plotline. Do you want to be the hero? Then get ready for some falling rocks. Brace for impact. And aren't we excited for it?

The good news? You're stronger than you know, and you discover it when the rocks fall before you. You're braver than you know, and you unsheathe it when the dragons rear back their heads. You're much more capable than you know, and you sharpen it when the hammer drops.

Every challenge, where you find yourself complaining or blaming, offers you the opportunity to become the best version of you. Greet those dragons with a brief nod, then rage onward--with kindness, courage, grit, and hope. Yes, you can.

***

Deuteronomy 31:6 says, "Be strong and courageous; don't be terrified or afraid of them. For it is the Lord your God who goes with you; He will not leave you or forsake you."

What is one challenge you find yourself battling today?

How can you see this verse being true in your situation?

What is one way that you can remind yourself of this truth and live this in your circumstances?

***

The Spirit of the Lord God is on Me, because the Lord has anointed Me to bring good news to the poor. He has sent Me to heal the brokenhearted, to proclaim liberty to the captives and freedom to the prisoners; to proclaim the year of the Lord's favor, and the day of our God's vengeance; to comfort all who mourn, to provide for those who mourn in Zion; to give them a crown of beauty instead of ashes, festive oil instead of mourning, and splendid clothes instead of despair.
Isaiah 61:1-3a

How can you see this verse being true in your situation?

What is one way that you can remind yourself of this truth and live this in your circumstances?

Earthshine

I accepted the document, two sweaty palms reaching, tentative, unprepared. I scanned the words, reading them aloud. "I've got this deep wrestling within my dark soul. A hunger for the oppressed. An almighty beckoning for the broken and bent, a writhing which cannot be tamed by silence. No; the silence, the hush, the hustle, cannot squelch the fire to share light for those trembling in the depths. I cannot stop giving of myself for my mission, for to stop is to suffocate. To quit, impossible. To surrender, unattainable. My wrestling therefore occurs not in the loss, but the gain. Loss no longer exists. All movement, all attempts, fulfill the mission. My mission.

"For I have been redeemed, and I defeat the darkness within me by each lent hand and rescued soul whom I reach. I am Alliance. I defend freedom, defy injustice, and deepen creative productivity to enhance mankind's survival. In living victory, I bear my burden, a warrior for my objective: Be powerful. Be consistent. Never quit. Finish the mission."

My eyes glanced up from the words to the Commander, then back down, reading, re-reading. Recoiling. Rerouting. "I guess with this kind of mission statement, there's no room for fear."

"There's no need for fear," he said. "It's not part of the mission."

"I am Alliance. I like it."

"I am Alliance."

"Hoo-rah."

(Excerpt from EARTHSHINE
by Kadee Carder)

***

When the Pharisees heard that He had silenced the Sadducees, they came together. And one of them, an expert in the law, asked a question to test Him: "Teacher, which command in the law is the greatest?"

Jesus said to him, "Love the Lord your God with all your heart, with all your soul, and with all your mind. This is the greatest and most important command. The second is like it: Love your neighbor as yourself. All the Law and the Prophets depend on these two commands."

Matthew 22:34-40

The book of Matthew follows Jesus from his birth, throughout his ministry and travels and interactions, his death, his resurrection, and his great commission to those who loved him. In my writing, travels, seeking, parenting, cooking, cleaning, gym sweating, and paper grading, there are times when I find myself asking, "What's the point?" Perhaps it comes out as, "What's the goal?" or "What's the purpose?" or "What's the mission statement?"

What's the one reason that fuels the 'why am I doing this'?

Having a mission statement helps.

The Bible will speak to each of us differently, for it is alive and active. The Holy Spirit meets us where we are and guides us. What burns in my heart may not interest you at all. What you find to be absolutely spot-on may not resonate as much with me. In all the years and all the words Jesus invested on earth, these seem to me as "the point." These are the mission statement. Why do we seek God? Why do we get up every morning? Why do we step forth with kindness and zeal? To love the Lord with heart, soul, mind. To love the Lord with all your energy, all your knowledge, all your power. To love the Lord with your actions, your thoughts, your life experiences. To live love by action, by faith, by staying focused on the mission. The mission, Jesus' mission, was not to display that he could heal, that he could turn rocks into bread, that he could control the weather, the crowds, or the authorities. Jesus came to redeem.

"Jesus did miracles to show people he loved them, not to show off how powerful he was. Jesus wasn't impressed with power; he is impressed by faith" (David Bryant).

In Book Five of the INSURRECTION series, my characters needed to revisit what they were doing. The Alliance Military Guard board of directors had met with conflict and chaos, and Commander McConnell finally realized that they needed to revisit their mission statement. Were they an organization built to destroy or to defend? Who were they protecting? Were they serving? Why did the Guard exist?

Perhaps you are focused and on-track. Perhaps you live in a sea of cupcakes, thorn-free roses, and have never stepped on a stray Lego. Or perhaps you find yourself wrestling the next choice, the next challenge, the current war.

The definition of "redeem" is to, "gain or regain possession of (something) in exchange for payment."

You have been redeemed.

Now the next question is…what are you doing with it?

***

Through the years spent writing the INSURRECTION series and agonizing hours trying to market books, I found myself let down. I couldn't find acceptable, tangible success. Blow by blow, each step I'd attempt to progress as an author met with resistance after resistance. The rejection and failure ate away at my spirit. It seemed like nobody cared. And from the ashes of broken dreams, from the depths of dark nights, of agony, of restlessness, of inability to wait with inaction, the story of EARTHSHINE came to be. Could a girl who's "done the hard thing" once more rise to the occasion? You see, there is not just one "hard thing" to face in life. There will be one, then another, and another. Each time more difficult, each time more unhinged and chaotic, each time drawing the protagonist further into the hero position. What would Saylor do when asked to face her greatest fears, knowing they are real?

I wasn't ready to write EARTHSHINE when the words began spilling out. It began with another title – Deadlight.

Halfway through, exploring the theme and tone generated by the title "dead-light," the word no longer fit. Is death the finale? While it served as an intriguing vocabulary word, no, it didn't fit with Saylor and Tucker's story. Theirs is a story of perseverance, of love, of hope. Of reflection. Of audacity. Of moxie. Of grit. One morning as I began to wrap up the final chapters on my manuscript, my "Word of the Day" email popped into my inbox. The term, "earthshine," lit up my screen. In fact, it lit up my eyes from its first appearance, because earthshine means…well…I suppose you'll have to read the book to find out.

I hope you will.

I hope you enjoy the story that had to be written.

I hope you may also get back up, once your heart has broken.

I hope you will be the one who shows up, builds up, and believes.

May you be the light, shining into the abyss. May you focus on the mission. May you be someone's Earthshine.

***

Which of the elements of loving God (heart, soul, mind, strength) is hardest for you to live out? Why?

What is one action you can take today to love the Lord your God with all your heart, soul, mind, and strength?

The Ruling Three

All people possess a cup of wrath, a yoke, and a cross to bear. Let's start with the cross to bear. You've got some great, burning desire that you cannot turn away or quell. It's some kind of creation, some kind of sturdy resonating within your chest. That's your thing that you're here to do. Maybe you understand the end goal for that cross, but I think most of us continually pursue that cross. The cross alludes to Jesus dying on the cross--he came to earth to seek and to save what was lost. He came to free us. He came to give us life. By fulfilling his purpose on the cross, he set the prisoners free. He faced the ultimate fear and loosed the bliss of humanity. Will your cross be painful? Yes. Will it be absolutely 100% worth it? Absolutely. Don't think about the pain of it--focus on the bliss it fulfills. Focus on the good that cross does. All good things cost. The best work comes after high costs from the creator. That's the hero plotline.

The yoke is the actual job and task of doing the work. The yoke includes the people you must deal with in order to accomplish your tasks. Your yoke consists of your family, your neighbors, your peers, every life you touch. The yoke consists of the means to doing and accomplishing your work.

The cup of wrath simply means that because you are alive, you will face trials. BUT! "In this world you will have trouble," Jesus said. "But take heart! I have overcome the world!" Where you can see trouble, challenge, or frustration as a chance to whine, face it with gratitude. Instead of asking "Why isn't this easier?" ask, "How can this make me better?" Here you have every opportunity to become the hero.

These three things every human possesses, the cross, the yoke, the cup, are the beautiful trinity of why we're here. Why are you here? What's your rule of three? "Life happens for you, not to you" (Byron Katie). Can you see how it's a fulfillment of your best life?

Believe in yourself, your Alliance, and seeing failure as an opportunity for growth. In my INSURRECTION books, the Alliance Military Guard serves as a rally point, deploying soldiers across the globe to serve and protect. They're a privatized group whose board of directors got a little off track and divided up--half operated on the goal of achieving power, while the other half sought service, research, and the advancement of human capability. Saylor had to decide if she trusted her Commander to guide and guard her. She had to decide to follow orders and what directive she needed to take. So do you. Can you trust your Commander? Who *is* your Commander? You have one. Can you trust your Alliance? Your alliance aligns with your yoke. While you're doing your work, do you believe in all that of which you are capable? You are powerful. You are loving. You have an intellectual mind. You can walk among giants.

And when we fall down? When we sigh in frustration? When my arms fall to my sides under the weight? When my knees slam against the dirt? I listen to it. I study the stumble. I analyze the instigator of the darkness. I listen to the shadows and seek the truth. Then I go back to the important "rule of three" and decide how I can do better next time. Did I focus on my business? Did I focus on my cross? Did I stay humble? Did I do my best? How can I do better next time?

"Life happens for you, not to you" (Byron Katie). Life serves you, for your hero journey. We know this, because God's got his business, and his business put you here in your time and space. He's given you your yoke, your cup, and your cross. He's your Alliance, your Commander, who gave you marching orders. He wants you to be the hero. Remember he said, *"Come to Me, all of you who are weary and burdened, and I will give you rest. All of you, take up My yoke and learn from Me, because I am gentle and humble in heart, and you will find rest for yourselves. For My yoke is easy and My burden is light"* (Matthew 11:28-30). He's right there beside you, the iron in your bones, helping you do that good work. It's quite beautiful and exciting, isn't it? Now, get back to the mission. Adventure awaits.

***

What weight rests upon your shoulders right now?

At that time Jesus said, "I praise You, Father, Lord of heaven and earth, because You have hidden these things from the wise and learned and revealed them to infants. Yes, Father, because this was Your good pleasure. All things have been entrusted to Me by My Father. No one knows the Son except the Father, and no one knows the Father except the Son and anyone to whom the Son desires to reveal Him. Come to Me, all of you who are weary and burdened, and I will give you rest. All of you, take up My yoke and learn from Me, because I am gentle and humble in heart, and you will find rest for yourselves. For My yoke is easy and My burden is light."
Matthew 11:25-30

What does this say to you?

How do you rest in God?

What is one thing that you can do today to rest in God?

Author Bio - Kadee Carder

Fierce yet sparkly, she rallies seekers to thrive in their stories. The goal is magic, the medium is ink, and the fuel is coffee. And sometimes pizza. She teaches English on the university level when she's not dancing around the living room with her family, lifting heavy at the gym, traveling the planet, or binging superhero shows.

INSURRECTION, INCOMPLETE, INDELIBLE, HERE BE DRAGONS, EARTHSHINE and non-fiction inspirational KINGDOM COME roll out perilous motives, twisty plots, and daring protagonists. Grab some real estate and your copy of her latest adventure and follow along on KadeeCarder.com.

Facebook: *https://www.facebook.com/kadeecarderink*
Instagram: @kadeecarderink

About
Harry Potter

Harry Potter has become one of the best-selling works of our age. It became a classic in just a few short years after publication. It has sold more than 400 million copies and been translated into 68 languages making it into the top three most-sold works in the world through the last 50 years (The Bible, in first place, has sold nearly 4 billion copies in that same amount of time.)

J. K. Rowling's popular story is about an orphan boy who, when he turns eleven, discovers that he has magical powers and abilities and is sent to study magic at a special school. The normal world neither knows of the magic world nor understands it. Through the course of his adventures, Harry discovers his family history and destiny, deep friendships, and true purpose as he struggles with a dark enemy who has been trying to eliminate his family since even before Harry's birth. That simplified synopsis sounds rife with talking points to relate to Scripture!

Dreaming Your Life Away

"Those who work their land will have abundant food, but those who chase fantasies will have their fill of poverty."
Proverbs 28:19

Dreams and imagination are good things. Considering what might be possible is the path to new inventions and better methods of accomplishing things. It's how we make progress, in our own lives and as a society.

But dreams can easily produce the opposite effect. The enticing ideas of what we hope for, outside of what already exists, can lead to envy, irresponsibility, and laziness. How often do people plan out how they'll spend money that they assume they'll win from the lottery or a sales bonus, only to find themselves in deep debt when their dream income doesn't arrive? How many people plan details of their wedding before they've even met someone they want to share their life with? How many people expect to have their talents "discovered" and achieve overnight stardom? When dreams become more important to us than reality, they become dangerous, dragging us off into a dream world where nothing is actually accomplished.

In *Harry Potter and the Sorcerer's Stone,* Harry Potter discovers a strange mirror, in which he sees a reflected image of his long dead parents, smiling at him. Harry never knew them, since they were both slain by the evil sorcerer, Voldemort, when Harry was an infant. When Harry shows the standing mirror to his best friend, Ron, the image of Harry's parents cannot be seen. Instead, Ron sees himself as an outstanding success, having become Head Boy and captain of the school Quidditch team. Harry can't understand why they see different images, but the school headmaster, Professor Dumbledore, soon clears things up.

"Let me explain. The happiest man on earth would be able to use the Mirror of Esired like a normal mirror, that is, he would look into it and see himself exactly as he is. Does that help?"

Harry thought. Then he said slowly, "It shows us what we want ... whatever we want ..."

"Yes and no," said Dumbledore quietly. "It shows us nothing more or less than the deepest, most desperate desire of our hearts. You, who have never known your family, see them standing around you. Ronald Weasley, who has always been overshadowed by his brothers, sees himself standing alone, the best of all of them. However, this mirror will give us neither knowledge or truth. Men have wasted away before it, entranced by what they have seen, or been driven mad, not knowing if what it shows is real or even possible.

"The Mirror will be moved to a new home tomorrow, Harry, and I ask you not to go looking for it again. If you ever do run across it, you will now be prepared. It does not do to dwell on dreams and forget to live, remember that."

If Harry had examined the mirror itself more closely, he might have figured out for himself what it reveals, by reading the mirror's inscription backwards and with the spaces rearranged:

erised stra ehru oyt ube cafru oyt on wohsi.

But the lure of a dream can easily paralyze us into adopting a dreamlike state, wishing and hoping for something to magically happen, instead of acting to make it happen while also enjoying other aspects of life. And in that stupor, we often fail to notice details of the reality around us.

If we use our dreams to propel us to action, we can change our reality for the better. Instead of wasting away, doing nothing but dreaming, we can turn our dreams into goals, and schedule time for pursuing them, without ignoring the rest of our responsibilities in life. We should never stop dreaming of better thing for our lives and the lives of others. But we shouldn't sacrifice the life we already have for the life we wish for.

Cherish your dreams and make them your starting place, not your ending place.

Now listen, you who say, "Today or tomorrow we will go to this or that city, spend a year there, carry on business and make money." Why, you do not even know what will happen tomorrow. What is your life? You are a mist that appears for a little while and then vanishes. Instead, you ought to say, "If it is the Lord's will, we will live and do this or that."
James 4:13-15

The Words We Believe

"For he chose us in him before the creation of the world to be holy and blameless in his sight. In love he predestined us for adoption to sonship through Jesus Christ, in accordance with his pleasure and will."
Ephesians 1: 4-5

Has anyone ever said something nasty about you? Some hurtful comment that stuck with you for years, perhaps even to this day?

Of course they have. Everyone has been labeled as stupid, ugly, careless, cruel, or any number of other terrible things. When people criticize us, it's easy to believe them, and hard to shake the thought that those criticisms were true.

In *Harry Potter and the Sorcerer's Stone,* ten-year old Harry Potter has been taken in by the Dursleys, his relatives who refuse to allow anything too unusual in their lives. They love their son, Dudley, and shower him with attention and gifts: thirty-nine gifts on his birthday, to be exact. But they force Harry to sleep in a small, dusty cupboard beneath the stairs. Then they order him to cook the family's breakfast, while they continually accuse him of doing terrible things. Strange things have always happened around Harry, but he has no idea why, or why the Dursleys keep acting as though he caused the bizarre happenings. After Mrs. Dursley gives him a bad haircut, his hair somehow grows back to its normal length by morning. When he tries to escape some bullies, he somehow ends up on the roof of a school building.

The truth, of course, is that Harry is a wizard. A truth that frightens and disgusts the Dursleys. So instead of revealing this, they continue to suppress the truth, and try to persuade Harry that he is to blame for these strange occurrences.

They try to convince him that he is a bad child.

But then, letters start coming to Harry. So many letters, appearing again and again no matter how often the Dursleys shred them. Harry wants to read them but the Dursleys refuse to let him. Instead, they flee, hoping no one can find them to send any more of the letters.

But an enormous man carrying an umbrella, Hagrid, does find Harry and reveals to him the he is a wizard, and the letters contain his invitation to practice magic at Hogwarts School of Witchcraft and Wizardry. Harry is speechless, certain that Hagrid has made a mistake in thinking he's a wizard. All his life he's been told that he's not special or important, so that is what he has come to believe.

But Hagrid, and the letters, say something different.

There are letters written about you, too. Letters that tell us that God loved us so much he gave his only son to save us from the condemnation we deserve. Letters that tell us God has blessed us with everything we need for life and godliness. Letters that say Jesus will never leave us or forsake us.

It's easy to let the harmful words of others define us. We can view ourselves in the same negative way, believing that every criticism they spoke about us is true.

But if God loved us enough to give himself for us, doesn't that prove we're extremely valuable to God? If God raised Jesus from the dead and that same holy power lives in us, doesn't that demonstrate that God can rescue and lead us into great things?

Don't buy into the lies that you don't matter, or that you only cause trouble, or that you have nothing significant to offer people. Your kindness, joy, patience, love, and hope can transform everyone around you. Instead of listening to the criticism of others, find out what God says about you. Read his letters and know that you are precious in God's sight.

Choosing Who To Become

"Therefore, if anyone is in Christ, he is a new creation. The old has passed away; behold, the new has come."
II Corinthians 5:17

Do you ever feel doomed? Destined to fail, or to fall to temptation, no matter how hard you try to do what's right? Do you feel as if the cards of life are stacked against you? That you can never succeed, because of the environment in which you were raised, or the bad choices of the people who raised you, or your own bad choices? Do you feel like there's no hope for you?

Harry Potter felt that way, in *Harry Potter and the Chamber of Secrets,* when he discovered that he shared a strange gift with the evil sorcerer, Voldemort. The ability to talk to snakes.

When other kids see that Harry can speak to snakes – even command them – they fear that he might be the Heir of Slitherin, destined to open the Chamber of Secrets, and unleash a monster that will devour all the children who are not considered to be of purely magical heritage. Since Salazar Slitherin lived so long ago, it's possible that Harry really is his heir. And given his odd communication with snakes, he wonders if he might actually be evil. Especially since the Sorting Hat, which assigns students to their shared houses, almost assigned him to the house of Slitherin when he first came to Hogwarts school.

Harry later discovers that Voldemort was once a student at Hogwarts, who had a terrible home life, and who lied to Professor Dumbledore about his secret knowledge instead of seeking help. Just like Harry.

Perhaps he really was evil.

In the end, Harry triumphs over Voldemort's latest scheme, when the same Sorting Hat appears, bringing Harry a sword to use in battle against a giant beast. Harry later tells Dumbledore about his fears of being evil. Dumbledore asks Harry why the Sorting Hat placed him in the Gryffindor house instead of Slitherin. Harry says it is because he asked the hat to place him there. Dumbledore points out that this choice makes Harry very different from Voldemort, even though they share some abilities and character traits.

"It is our choices, Harry, that show what we truly are, far more than our abilities," Dumbledore tells him. Then he shows him the proof. The sword that Harry had pulled from the Sorting Hat for his final battle is inscribed with the name of his house's founder, Godric Gryffindor. "Only a true Gryffindor could have pulled that out of the hat," Dumbledore says.

Sharing the same family DNA, the same town, the same social group, or even the same interests as others does not make us the same as them. These shared qualities are simply that, and do not define our identity. We are free in Christ to honor God and bless others, because that is what God has called us to do. We can choose, and those choices will make us who we are.

Being There

"To the weak I become weak, to win the weak. I have become all things to all people so that by all possible means I might save some."

I Corinthians 9:22

Sometimes, in order to help someone, you have to go where that person is. Even if that means going to an uncomfortable place. Like a neighbor's smelly apartment. Or a family member's court hearing. Or a friend's struggle to break a shameful addiction.

It's easy to keep our distance from those people who make us feel awkward, or who are suffering through difficult problems. It's hard to commit to helping someone when we know it might cost us a lot of time, sleep, resources, or even our reputation with others who don't want us associating with such people.

In *Harry Potter and the Prisoner of Azkaban,* we learn that the admirable Professor Lupin has a dark and dangerous secret. He's a werewolf, and has been so since he was a student at Hogwart's. Fortunately, his closest friends decided to stay with him during every full moon when he transformed into a wolf. They cast spells on themselves, to turn each of them into an animagus – a person who can transform from human to animal form. They each chose their own animal and nickname. "Wormtail", a rat; "Padfoot", a dog; and "Prawns", a stag – to join Lupin, nicknamed "Moony". Whenever Lupin became a wolf, the others would join him and keep him from harming others, while also keeping him company on long, lonely nights.

It was uncomfortable. It was dangerous.

It was the high price of true friendship.

Jesus said, *"Greater love has no one than this: to lay down one's life for one's friends." (John 15:13)* Lupin's friends could not have done anything more to demonstrate their devotion, than to be with him in his most shameful and loathsome state. Not to judge or correct or fix. Simply to be present, and share his burden.

To be his friend through the worst times of his life.

Is there someone in your life that God is calling you to comfort right now, in their most difficult struggles? To know, in their darkest times, that they are not alone? To see that they are truly loved?

Who can you encourage today, simply by being there?

Crying Out

"Awake, Lord! Why do you sleep?

Rouse yourself! Do not reject us forever.

Why do you hide your face and forget our misery and oppression?

We are brought down to the dust; our bodies cling to the ground.

Rise up and help us; rescue us because of your unfailing love."

Psalms 44:23-26

Many of the Harry Potter fans who read the fifth book, *Harry Potter and the Order of the Phoenix,* asked the same question: Why is Harry so angry in this book?

Author J. K. Rowling later revealed that she was pregnant when she wrote it, and her publisher kept pressuring her to finish it, so her own irritability came across through Harry.

We can all relate to the feeling of being overwhelmed in life. Even Harry. After all the horrors he's experienced, he has every right to be irritable. Even if he's normally more resilient and cheerful, at some point, the pressures of life wear us all down.

In *Harry Potter and the Order of the Phoenix,* the pressure mounts on Harry, but he finds less and less support. First, he is summoned to appear in court by the Ministry of Magic, who oversees all magic use. As an underage wizard, Harry is not allowed to use magic outside of his school, and he is put on trial for doing so. He claims it was in self-defense against Dementors, dangerous magical creatures who threatened him and his cousin, but the Ministry refuses to believe him. In fact, they seem intent on prosecuting him without a fair trial. Thankfully, Harry's wise mentor, Professor Dumbledore, arrives in time to give testimony and rescue Harry. But before Harry can thank him, Dumbledore abruptly leaves without a word. Not even taking the time to say "hello".

Returning to Hogwarts school, Harry learns that another reliable friend, Hagrid, is not there this year, and no one seems to know why. Meanwhile, most of the students think Harry is lying about witnessing the return of the evil sorcerer, Voldemort. So does a new teacher, Professor Umbridge, who has been sent by the Ministry to help observe the activities of Hogwarts. But she soon starts taking over the school, issuing strict rules and punishments and telling everyone that Harry is a liar. Even worse, Harry feels that something is taking over his own mind, as Voldemort's thoughts seem to invade his own, making him short-tempered and hostile. He longs to lean on his usual friends for support, but Hagrid is missing and Professor Dumbledore refuses to even acknowledge him. To the point that Harry finally shouts at Dumbledore, demanding that he look at him and explain what's happening to his mind.

Dumbledore recruits Professor Snape to train Harry to resist Voldemort's attempts to invade Harry's mind.

Dumbledore later reveals that he had to keep his distance to prevent Voldemort from spying on him through Harry. He hated to leave Harry on his own, but he couldn't risk Voldemort learning their plans to defeat him.

Sometimes life is overwhelming, and no one seems to be available to help. Sometimes, no matter how hard we pray, how much we read the Bible, or how much wise advice we receive, we simply cannot handle life's burdens. This is why we have books in the Bible like *Psalms,* which often shows God's people pouring out their confusion and complaints, crying out to God for relief.

Not that we should presume to vent our anger or complaints at God with disrespect or a lack of reverence for his authority and his kindness. But we can come to God in our frustration, because God knows that we, as children, can't always understand why we must endure suffering or disappointment. So we complain and cry.

And God, as a good father, listens. Bigger than our complaints, fears, and problems.

When life becomes overwhelming, and all you can feel is pain, remember that God is still our loving father, and his shoulders are always big enough for us to cry on.

Author Bio - D.A. Randall

D. A. Randall studied acting at Judson University, learning how to create compelling characters and powerful stories through acting techniques. He served for 9 years afterward as Drama Director at his local church, writing weekly dramas and teaching acting and storytelling basics to adult volunteers. He now writes action thrillers that read like blockbuster movies. Action-packed, fast-paced & fun, with larger than life heroes facing off against diabolical villains as they struggle through deep moral dilemmas. His stories are published as Character Entertainment – building character through fiction, with stories that demonstrate courage, friendship, acceptance, faith, honor, and self-sacrifice.

You can find his books on Amazon, Barnes & Noble, and other online booksellers. You can also subscribe to his newsletter for advance alerts of new stories at *www.RandallAllenDunn.com*.

About
The Red Rider Saga

The Red Rider saga is a paranormal action series about a 16-year old Red Riding Hood battling the Lycanthru, a cult of werewolves bent on seizing the French throne.

After a wolf scarred her face in childhood, Helena Basque was plagued by nightmares and local bullies. She learned how to hunt and fight in order to defend herself. Now at age sixteen, she determines that none will rise up to stop the deadly wolf attacks, and she decides to destroy them herself. Donning a red hooded cloak like the one she was forbidden to wear in childhood, Helena arms herself with a repeating crossbow that uses silver-tipped bolts. She soon strikes fear in the hearts of the wolves and is the legendary heroine they call "the Red Rider".

As she continues waging her personal war, Helena learns who she can genuinely trust among both old and new friends. She also learns to sacrifice her own desires for a normal life in order to stand up for what's right and protect people from the wolves. In the end, she learns that she is neither isolated nor unattractive, but loved by close friends who treat her like family.

Nothing Alike

"For there is no difference between Jew and Gentile – the same Lord is Lord of all and richly blesses all who call on him."
Romans 10:12

Concerned about her social life, Helena's mother suggests something that is far out of her daughter's comfort zone: she urges Helena to make friends with other girls in town, such as Celia Verdante.

Helena laughs hard. She has absolutely nothing in common with Celia, the rich and beautiful snob who obsesses about fancy clothes and parties. In fact, Helena finds proof of this after she starts battling the wolves, when she overhears Celia mocking her. Celia agrees with the local rumors that Helena has lost her mind, acting like a savage animal, dressing in men's trousers and spending every night in the woods. She considers Helena an insult to femininity and suggests that she wears the red hood to hide her marred face. Hearing this, Helena feels justified in her decision not to take her mother's advice and give Celia a chance.

It's easy to distance ourselves from certain people who don't seem to share our basic values. The very idea of associating with such people is almost laughable. Why would we? While Celia detests Helena and looks down on her, Helena has an equal distaste for Celia. Even if Celia showed kindness, Helena might feel uncomfortable around someone who looks and dresses so much fancier than she does, and who has such different interests and priorities in life.

Yet Jesus associated with the sort of people that society rejected: blind and lame beggars, corrupt tax collectors, diseased lepers, lewd prostitutes. Every meeting with one of these people cost Jesus his social standing. This was one of Jesus's habits that the Pharisees could not understand. But Jesus remained open, even to the Pharisees. The famous gospel summation in John 3:16 is from his conversation with Nicodemus, a Pharisee who came to learn more about his teachings, and who later helped bury his body. There was no sort of person whom Jesus rejected. Not even us. While Jesus was completely sinless, he loved and died for us while we were still sinners. And his prayer for his disciples and for us was that we will be united as one, like he was and is one with God, the Father. God wants to draw us to himself, and draw us to one another, in spite of our differences.

Later on, after Helena rescues Celia from one of the wolves, she asks Celia to create a disguise to help her infiltrate the royal ball. Celia still finds Helena repulsive, but she knows she owes Helena her life. She agrees to tailor a dress for her, even applying makeup to hide Helena's scars. Seeing how beautiful Celia has made her, Helena is stunned. She realizes this is the joy that her mother wanted for her, to have fun in life, dressing up and attending parties with friends. But she shoves those longings aside, knowing she has a job to do. As Celia escorts her into the ball, finessing her way past the guards to smuggle in Helena's weapons, Helena discovers that Celia is not merely a vapid socialite, as she assumed. She is brave, skilled, and willing to risk her life for what's right. Under pressure, she is not so different from Helena after all. Celia also gains a fresh respect for Helena. Though she can't see herself associating with Helena as a friend, she knows Helena is the only one protecting their community from the wolves, perhaps in the only way it can be done. Over time, her respect for Helena grows more and more, as she realizes that Helena's way of doing things might not be so repulsive after all, given the situation. Meanwhile, Helena begins to trust Celia more and more, not as a mere acquaintance or even a friend, but as an ally.

Instead of focusing on what separates us from some people, let's focus on what might unite us. Others who seem so different from us might share the same desire for justice, mercy, friendship, and hope that we have. And if we can't see those shared values right away, let's go hunting for them, and give one another a chance.

Stand Up and Do Something

"In the same way, faith by itself, if it is not accompanied by action, is dead."
James 2:17

One of my favorite sayings is, "Anything worth doing is worth doing poorly." Reading that might make you look twice. Isn't it supposed to say, "… is worth doing *well?"* Why would someone want to do something poorly?

So that it gets done.

Wait, are you saying that it's acceptable to do a poor job, instead of doing the best you can do? I'm not suggesting that we be lazy, or careless, or flippant in our efforts. I'm simply saying that, most of the time, we need to overcome our personal fears and take action. The biggest fear most of us face is the fear of failure. We expect to fail, so we never try. This gets compounded by the false belief that we must always do excellent work. We should certainly do our best, but if we're ill, or if we lack certain education or skills, or if we're overly busy with parenting or planning major events, then the best work we can do might not be excellent. But it can still be good, and very effective.

Yet most of us never try because we think our results need to be "excellent".

In other words, perfect.

So we put off learning a new skill. After all, it's difficult to learn, and what if we never learn to do it well enough? We avoid meeting new people. What if they don't like us? We even hesitate to help others who obviously need it. What if we mess up?

In *The Red Rider,* sixteen-year-old Helena Basque must overcome her own fears in order to help herself and her community. She knows there are strange wolves attacking people, but the French government refuses to send help and no local authorities can combat them. Helena has learned how to hunt well, and even fight, but she is still only a young girl. Worse, she's a young girl who is bullied because of the scars on her face from a childhood wolf attack. Her disfigurement causes a local bully, Jacque Denue, to harass her, as he and his friends call Helena an ugly witch and order her to stop coming to town.

She looks up to her hero, Francois, the woodcutter who saved her life from the wolf that wounded her. But Francois tells her that a hero isn't always someone who's brave or strong. It's simply someone who sees a need and chooses to stand up and do something about it. She remembers his words a few years later, when Jacque Denue and his buddies chase her down an alley and start throwing rocks at her, leaving her no place to run. Deciding to "stand up and do something", she faces her fear, grabbing a wooden plank to swat away the rocks they keep hurling. Until she faces Jacque and beats him to the ground, no longer afraid of him.

She later determines to hunt the wolves that terrorize their province, since no one else is attempting to stop them. In the process, she discovers the wolves' plans and their weaknesses, and soon becomes a deadly threat to them. But she started out with no real plan. Just a determination to succeed, and to do something that needed to be done.

To stand up and do something.

You don't have to be the strongest or smartest or the most talented. You don't even have to know how to do what you set out to do. A journey of a thousand miles starts with a single step. The most difficult part is usually overcoming the fears that keep us from starting.

Take that step.

Everything You Need

"His divine power has given us everything we need for a godly life through our knowledge of him who called us by his own glory and goodness."
2 Peter 1:3

Helena is used to fighting evil Lycanthru wolves with her weapons. In fact, it's a large part of what makes her such a serious threat to them, once she discovered that silver-edged weapons kill them within seconds. With her repeating crossbow loaded with ten silver-tipped bolts, she can easily dispose of several wolves in succession. Combined with her silver blades and the red-hooded cloak that identifies her as the one who can destroy them, Helena can easily hold her own against an entire wolf pack.

But then she is captured and forced to fight the wolves without her cloak and weapons. She can't imagine surviving against these monsters without her defensive weapons. She can only expect certain defeat, suffering, and humiliation.

Until she realizes that she isn't helpless. True, she can't fight the way she normally would. But she remembers she can still fight, the way her mentor instructed her long ago. Using the wolves' momentum and their own weapons against them, she manages to not only survive, but turn the tide against her enemies. She had come to rely so heavily on her usual methods of attack that she had forgotten how much strength and skill she possessed without them.

The Bible tells about a similar situation, when a group of Israelites approached their leader, Joshua, with a problem. After the Israelites finally obtained the land that God promised them, the tribes of Manasseh and Ephraim insisted that Joshua provide them with more land because they were such a numerous people. Instead of giving in, Joshua encouraged them to use their strength to solve their own dilemma. He told them that because they were a numerous people, they should clear trees and overcome neighboring armies to develop more land for themselves. They balked at this, but Joshua insisted they would succeed and obtain more than enough land, by using their strength of numbers.

When overwhelmed by major problems, we can feel as helpless as those tribes, unable to recognize our own strength to solve them. Losing a job, mending a broken relationship, or completing a major project with limited time or resources can seem like insurmountable tasks. It's easier to sit and wait for a fresh miracle to do our work for us than to find ways to fix it ourselves.

When we feel overwhelmed, it's usually because we can't see a solution ourselves. We've exhausted all of our own ideas and efforts. That's when God wants us to seek help. By asking him to give us fresh wisdom to see the skills, resources, and people that he's already provided us. By having the humility to ask for help and guidance from family and friends who can solve a problem that's too challenging for us.

If you're facing a problem that seems unsolvable, recognize that God is willing and eager to help rescue you from it. Take time to pray for help and wisdom. You may be surprised at the solutions God has already given you.

Seeing Our Scars

"I was given a thorn in my flesh, a messenger of Satan, to torment me. Three times I pleaded with the Lord to take it away from me. But he said to me, 'My grace is sufficient for you, for my power is made perfect in weakness.' Therefore I will boast all the more gladly about my weaknesses, so that Christ's power may rest on me. That is why, for Christ's sake, I delight in weaknesses, in insults, in hardships, in persecutions, in difficulties. For when I am weak, then I am strong."
2 Corinthians 12:7b-10

Helena hates her scars. Of all places to have ugly claw marks, she has them on her face. And they're huge. The three broad cuts tearing across her cheeks are impossible to ignore. Ever since she was marred by a wolf, she's felt ashamed to be around attractive, "normal" people.

But Pierre sees something different. He thinks Helena is beautiful. Of course, he knows that she's scarred, but he sees not only the beauty beneath the scars, but the beauty of the scars themselves.

This makes no sense to Helena. So Pierre shows her a silver figurine he designed of Diana, the Greek goddess of the hunt. He confesses he made a mistake that left part of the figure's head dented. In spite of this imperfection, and because of it, it's one of his favorite works. Seeing the figurine's flaw, Helena understands what he means. Its imperfection only draws attention to the masterful parts of the piece, while making the sculptor and the figurine seem more human, sharing the same flaws as other people. He tells Helena, "See, some scars make us more beautiful."

It's hard for us to celebrate our scars. We prefer to hide them, knowing how ugly they are to most people. Our sins, past

171

mistakes, and shortcomings make us feel unfit and unqualified among crowds of "normal" people.

But God sees something different. He not only sees who we are beneath our scarred lives, he sees how he is transforming those scars into something beautiful. The Bible shows us plenty of people whose scarred lives were transformed by God to make them into amazing heroes of the faith. Moses started out as a murderer and a fugitive. Samson was arrogant and immature. Jacob was a con artist. Rahab was a prostitute living among God's enemies. King David used his authority to steal a soldier's wife and have the man killed. Peter kept vacillating between his bold commitment to following Christ and his fears that led him to betray Christ. The apostle Paul hunted down Christians to arrest and sentence them to death. When we look at the type of people God chose to use, our own failures and flaws seem less repulsive. Not only can God transform our scars, he can make them part of our testimony to show the beauty of our new lives in him.

Not everyone will see the beauty in your scars, so it's okay to be cautious about who sees them. Just make sure you see what God sees, admiring the beauty in your life. Even in your scars.

The Perfect Dress

"Your beauty should not come from outward adornment, such as elaborate hairstyles and the wearing of gold jewelry or fine clothes. Rather, it should be that of your inner self, the unfading beauty of a gentle and quiet spirit, which is of great worth in God's sight."
I Peter 3: 3-4

Helena has never been able to see herself as pretty. Even though Pierre sees her that way and others admire her, she still knows she has facial scars that can never be removed. Which means that, at least in part, she will always be ugly and deformed.

Pierre's mother, Lisette, makes a new dress for Helena and insists she try it on. Helena is shocked to discover that the dress is not only beautiful, but it makes her feel stunning. Even her scars seem beautiful when wearing the dress, as if they are part of its design. And in fact, they are. Lisette knows Helena, and knows from personal experience how it feels to have a deformity, since she is blind in one eye. So she created a perfect dress for Helena that fit her features, even her scars. So much so that Helena believes the dress would be less attractive if a woman without scars wore it.

We often have trouble accepting our flaws. Especially the glaring ones, the ones that others can't help but notice. When we know we have such flaws, we tend to magnify them in our minds, imagining that other people only see our faults or limitations, rather than our strengths.

But sometimes the things we wish to change about ourselves are the things that actually help define our character, making us more attractive to others. We may be scarred, uneducated, poor at communicating, physically slow, or have any number of hindrances. But those limitations often highlight the more valuable parts of our character: our patience, perseverance, acceptance of others, or good listening skills. Sometimes our limits force us to master more important life skills that not only benefit us but are a great benefit to those around us.

After being surprised by the dress, Helena asked Father Vestille to tell her the honest truth of whether she's ugly. He's shocked by the question, assuring her that she is a very pretty girl, and that her scars have nothing to do with it. He tells her she could have chosen to become ugly, through bitterness over all the suffering she has endured. Instead, she chose to act bravely and selflessly to protect her community from the deadly wolves. He reminds her that the Scriptures teach young women not to adorn themselves with fine jewelry or braided hair, but with good deeds. Based on this, he assesses Helena as one of the most beautiful women in the province.

Are you seeing your genuine beauty, demonstrated by your heart and your actions? Because that's what God sees.

Author Bio - D.A. Randall

D. A. Randall studied acting at Judson University, learning how to create compelling characters and powerful stories through acting techniques. He served for 9 years afterward as Drama Director at his local church, writing weekly dramas and teaching acting and storytelling basics to adult volunteers. He now writes action thrillers that read like blockbuster movies. Action-packed, fast-paced & fun, with larger than life heroes facing off against diabolical villains as they struggle through deep moral dilemmas. His stories are published as Character Entertainment – building character through fiction, with stories that demonstrate courage, friendship, acceptance, faith, honor, and self-sacrifice.

You can find his books on Amazon, Barnes & Noble, and other online booksellers. You can also subscribe to his newsletter for advance alerts of new stories at *www.RandallAllenDunn.com*.

About
The Lunar
Chronicles

The next few devotions are based on The Lunar Chronicles, which puts a science fiction spin on the classic fairy tales of Cinderella, Little Red Riding Hood, Rapunzel, and Snow White. Most fairy tales were designed as morality tales, to teach powerful lessons about how to be wise, brave, kind, and loyal, and The Lunar Chronicles is no different.

In a future world that includes cyborgs and androids, Earth suffers through a Cold War with the hostile planet Luna, whose aliens wield the power to control people's minds and make themselves appear irresistibly beautiful. Their merciless ruler, Queen Levana, intends to dominate Earth, which is already weakened by a decimating plague called letumosis, for which Luna holds a possible cure.

Hope springs when a teenage cyborg mechanic named Linh Cinder discovers that she might have the power, and the duty, to stop Queen Levana. But her cruel stepmother and stepsisters barely allow her to have a life, let alone the freedom to start a revolution.

Later, young Scarlet Benoit seeks her missing grandmother, stopping at nothing to find her. Even if it means partnering with a suspicious street fighter named Wolf, who might have had something to do with her grandmother's kidnapping.

Cinder and Scarlet soon combine their forces in their fight. They are then joined by Cress, a brilliant young computer hacker forced to work for the Lunar Empire, and Winter, the Queen's daughter, who has gone half-insane from suppressing her Lunar power to control people's minds. These four young women and their friends fight for their lives and for the freedom of Earth in this powerful science fiction fairy tale epic. We can learn lessons for life from their bold example.

The Lunar Chronicles is a well-known series of young adult science fiction novels written by author Marissa Meyer. Each book entails a new take on an old fairy tale.

Cinder – Invaluable

"Here there is no Gentile or Jew, circumcised or uncircumcised, barbarian, Scythian, slave or free, but Christ is all, and is in all."
Colossians 3:11

Linh Cinder isn't like her family. In fact, she isn't like anyone she knows.

She's a cyborg. And in her world, cyborgs are treated as second-class citizens. Often feared, hated, and repellant to the rest of humanity.

Yet her cybernetic makeup has helped to make Cinder an excellent mechanic, even if she has to hide the secret of her intimate knowledge of machinery. If anyone knew what she really was … well, she would probably lose a lot of business, and perhaps much of her freedom.

Of course, her stepmother, Linh Adri, and her stepsisters know that she's a cyborg, and they consider her a disgusting burden. Which is why, when Cinder's stepsister, Linh Peony, contracts the deadly letumosis disease from a junkyard where she had accompanied Cinder, Linh Adri "volunteers" Cinder for laboratory experimentation, which hopes to find a cure for the decimating plague. It doesn't concern Linh Adri in the least that no one has survived any of these experiments. In fact, she trusts that she will never have to see Cinder again. She does not consider it murder, or even cruelty. Because she does not consider Cinder to be human.

This is a science fiction fairy tale, but such mindsets are not uncommon in reality. The Nazi empire rose primarily on the belief that Jews were to blame for many of society's problems and had to be exterminated. African-Americans have long been denied rights and opportunities and been suspected of crimes and murdered, simply because of their skin color. Prejudice – the act of "pre-judging" someone based on certain criteria – has been around for centuries, and will continue to be.

But we can overcome our natural tendency to assume the worst about others, or treat them as less valuable. It's natural to presume certain things about a person, based on their political or religious beliefs, their style of clothing or hair, or even their hobbies or the music they listen to. It's easy to divide ourselves into different groups that cannot interact with one another, presuming we can never relate to those from other groups.

But Christ called us to be a family, accepting one another in spite of our minor differences, and expecting the best from one another. Those who dress, talk, and think differently from us can still be our friends. And those who follow Christ are already family, no matter how different they appear on the surface.

Cinder later discovers that her genes contain the potential for finding a cure for the letumosis disease. We might never know how important a person might be if we presume to know their value before learning more about them. Can you think of people you have made presumptions about, that God might be calling you to connect with? Such a relationship – and such a person – might prove to be invaluable.

Cress - Called Out

"Brothers and sisters, think of what you were when you were called. Not many of you were wise by human standards; not many were influential; not many were of noble birth. But God chose the foolish things of the world to shame the wise; God chose the weak things of the world to shame the strong. God chose the lowly things of this world and the despised things – and the things that are not – to nullify the things that are, so that no one may boast before him. It is because of him that you are in Christ Jesus, who has become for us wisdom from God – that is, our righteousness, holiness and redemption."
I Corinthians 1:26-30

Carswell Thorne doesn't see himself as a hero.

And he shouldn't. There's nothing very heroic about him. He's vain, selfish, lustful, superficial, a thief, and not too skilled as a fighter or a pilot. And he knows it.

But Cress doesn't. She's loved him from afar and believes him to be the man of her dreams.

But Thorne knows that the man he believes her to be is just that: a dream. Cress became infatuated with Thorne and presumed him to have all the positive traits she longed for in a man. Kindness, sensitivity, bravery, and a willingness to make noble sacrifices. Thorne knows he is none of those things, and tries to convince Cress of the truth.

Still, she persists in believing that, deep down, Thorne has a good and brave heart, and is capable of great things. She believes it so much that, ultimately, Thorne starts to believe it, too. When they are stranded together in an African desert and Thorne becomes blind, he must humbly rely on Cress for help. Having always been a loner and rebel, he's not used to relying on someone as a partner.

Later, when Cress is kidnapped, Thorne hurries to rescue her, though he still can't see, risking his life to save her.

Sometimes we can't see our own potential or worth. We see our present circumstances and our past mistakes and assume there is nothing more to our lives or our identities.

But God sees something different. He sees the heroes we can become. When we close our eyes to our current limitations and our past failures, we can see with eyes of faith what God calls us to be.

God is not limited by who we are or were, or how little we have to offer. He simply calls us to believe and follow him, and let him form us into new people.

Have you let go of your own view of yourself and your abilities, to allow God room to make you who he calls you to be? We don't know what God can transform us into, and we don't need to know. All we need to do is trust and follow him. He is the potter, and we are his clay. As we trust and obey him, what we become is not up to us or our past, but up to God.

Be the person he has called you to be.

Winter – Showing Kindness

"Therefore, as God's chosen people, holy and dearly loved, clothe yourselves with compassion, kindness, humility, gentleness and patience. Bear with each other and forgive one another if any of you has a grievance against someone. Forgive as the Lord forgave you. And over all these virtues put on love, which binds them all together in perfect unity."
Colossians 3:12-14

Winter is a crazy person. As in, she's completely out of her mind.

And everyone loves her.

Of course, she's pretty, which can make someone popular. Despite the facial scars she bears from her abusive mother, Queen Levana. But that's not why people love her.

And of course, she's a princess, so the people of the planet Luna are expected to give her praise and adoration. But that's not why they love her, either. The Lunars obey her mother out of fear, but they have no such love for Queen Levana.

So what make Winter the darling of the people?

It's her kindness.

She's kind to everyone, and everything. In the midst of her strange mutterings, Winter speaks positive words of hope and encouragement. Of love and acceptance. Of friendship and appreciation. To everyone.

She offers kindness in a world of cruelty. Friendliness in a word of self-absorbed vanity. Peace and contentment in a world of violent acts and greed.

For the people of Luna, this is a rare gift. One they can all receive from their darling princess.

Do you know how valuable kindness can be?

A smile to a friend or co-worker can change their outlook for the rest of that day. a compliment can encourage a weary person to persevere. A show of forgiveness can re-direct the actions of someone who had planned to do evil.

Simple acts of love can transform everyone around you.

But it starts with your own heart, with fully receiving the love we have been shown in Christ. Knowing that he first loved us, when we were evil and unlovable, enables us to love others. Knowing how much we've been forgiven allows us to forgive other people's sins. Knowing that the all-powerful ruler of the universe is caring for us gives us the peace and security we need to care for those around us.

God loved us enough to die for us. And he'll never stop loving us, no matter what we do or how we fail. He'll never stop chasing us down with his love.

So smile. Be at peace. Be encouraged, Knowing how greatly you are loved.

Share the love you have received with others; build them up. It doesn't matter if you have ugly scars. It doesn't matter if you say strange things sometimes. You don't have to be beautiful, or strong, or smart, to influence those around you. You just have to love.

Don't underestimate the power of kindness. Your kindness can change your entire world.

Scarlet – Winning the Battle for Your Soul

"For if you live according to the flesh, you will die; but if by the Spirit you put to death the misdeeds of the body, you will live. For those who are led by the Spirit of God are the children of God. The Spirit you received does not make you slaves, so that you live in fear again; rather, the Spirit you received brought about your adoption to sonship. And by him we cry, 'Abba, Father.'"
Romans 8:13-15

Wolf doesn't expect anyone to trust him. He can't even trust himself.

He warns Scarlet not to trust him, either, when they meet. He's a street fighter, used to dealing with violent and unscrupulous people, and he doesn't want her to be part of that world. But Scarlet wants to find her grandmother, who has gone missing, and she'll do whatever it takes to get her back.

When Scarlet's estranged father returns and tells her he was also kidnapped and tortured, all he can tell her about his captors is that one of them had an unusual tattoo. The same tattoo that Wolf bears on his forearm.

Scarlet confronts Wolf about it, and he tells her he once belonged to an evil group which likely still holds her grandmother hostage. He offers to help her find her grandmother and bring her home safely.

As they search, Wolf and Scarlet start to fall in love. But when they finally reach a place where they expect to find her grandmother, Wolf betrays Scarlet and hands her over to the Lunar Guards who kidnapped her grandmother. Wolf honestly loves Scarlet and wants to help her, but he's in too deep. He's a Lunar Special Operative, under orders to use Scarlet to help uncover her grandmother's secrets for resisting Lunar mind control. Even worse, the Lunars have manipulated Wolf, engineering him to kill for them. When Wolf's brother, Ran, kills Scarlet's grandmother and then tries to kill Scarlet, Wolf fights and kills him instead. Wolf still wants to kill Scarlet himself afterward, but resists the urge somehow. Scarlet and Wolf later determine that his animal instinct to protect her, as his chosen mate, had overpowered his instinct to kill.

Sometimes we can become so entrenched in sinful habits that we believe we can never escape them. Our sins become a pattern, not only of actions but also of thoughts, which are extremely difficult to break.

Breaking that pattern starts with a firm choice. A decision to repent and pursue a righteous life that honors God. Once we make that choice, it becomes far easier to follow through. To change our usual routines, perhaps even some relationships, that we know will influence us toward destructive behavior. To read the Bible daily and pray for the Holy Spirit's continued help to resist and flee from sin. Jesus said that anyone who sins is a slave to sin, but that he came among us to set the prisoners free.

Our sinful tendencies battle against our desires to serve God. But through the Holy Spirit's power and our choice to serve God and others, we can win the battle for our souls.

Make that choice today, to decide the person you will be tomorrow.

Some People Get All the Grace

"But he answered one of them, 'I am not being unfair to you, friend. Didn't you agree to work for a denarius? Take your pay and go. I want to give the one who was hired last the same as I gave you. Don't I have the right to do what I want with my own money? Or are you envious because I am generous?'"
Matthew 20:13-15

One part of The Lunar Chronicles storyline really bothers me. It's the way everything ends for Cinder's cruel stepmother Linh Adri.

It ends well.

After Linh Adri had shown such prejudice toward Cinder for being a cyborg.

After she had forced Cinder to do all the work for the family and lived off the income without lifting a finger to help.

After blaming Cinder for any misfortune they suffer, treating her as a curse instead of a blessing.

After forcing Cinder to submit herself to dangerous experimentation that she didn't expect Cinder to survive.

After taking away her cybernetic leg, forcing Cinder to limp back and forth to work.

After urging Emperor Kai and others to treat Cinder as a hostile fugitive who threatened the entire nation.

After doing all that, Linh Adri receives a fortune. The financial security she's always wanted.

And Cinder is the one who gives it to her!

Cinder's late father created a device to help humans block the mind control of Lunars. Cinder points out that Linh Adri holds the patent, as the wife of her late father, and should be compensated with a royalty for the production and distribution of these devices, which will range in the millions, at least.

It's not fair.

It would be easy for Cinder to keep this from Linh Adri, who didn't even know about the device. And as the new ruler, Cinder could easily refuse to let Linh Adri benefit from the invention, after all the cruelty she suffered from her over the years.

But in spite of all Linh Adri's hatred and abuse toward her, Cinder allows her stepmother to receive a rich inheritance. Linh Adri doesn't deserve such a blessing. In fact, she deserves the opposite.

Like most of us, I have a really hard time accepting grace … for other people.

I'm all for receiving things I don't deserve for myself – love, acceptance, forgiveness, guidance, hope, blessings. But when I see other people getting it – people who have committed far worse sins and done far more damage to people – well, I just don't want them to receive too much. Unless, of course, I receive it first, if I've spent more time seeking to do what pleases God. If they're going to receive grace and help and miracles and blessings, shouldn't I receive far more for serving God longer?

Jesus talked about this tendency of ours, to think that some people deserve more grace than others. He told a parable about hired hands who started early in the day and worked a full shift, while others got hired late in the afternoon but received the same pay. When the early workers started grumbling, their employer reminded them they had agreed to work a full day for the wages he promised, and what he did with his own money was up to him.

The point?

Everybody gets the same grace. No matter how many horrible crimes they've committed. No matter how cruel they've been. No matter how hard or how long they've worked against God or his people.

So if God chooses to bless someone – even with material things in this life – should we evaluate their merit in receiving it? Should we decide if someone deserves a promotion, or a friendship, or an inheritance, or any other sort of blessing? Or can we be grateful that we have received the same undeserved grace, the same undeserved blessings from God himself, when we deserved to be separated from him forever for our sinful acts?

Choose today to be grateful to God for his amazing grace that has saved us all, and for the blessings he gives each one of us.

And be grateful that he's given it to other undeserving people, too.

Author Bio – D.A. Randall

D. A. Randall studied acting at Judson University, learning how to create compelling characters and powerful stories through acting techniques. He served for 9 years afterward as Drama Director at his local church, writing weekly dramas and teaching acting and storytelling basics to adult volunteers. He now writes action thrillers that read like blockbuster movies. Action-packed, fast-paced & fun, with larger than life heroes facing off against diabolical villains as they struggle through deep moral dilemmas. His stories are published as Character Entertainment – building character through fiction, with stories that demonstrate courage, friendship, acceptance, faith, honor, and self-sacrifice.

You can find his books on Amazon, Barnes & Noble, and other online booksellers. You can also subscribe to his newsletter for advance alerts of new stories at *www.RandallAllenDunn.com*.

Like What We Do?

Here are 13 ways you can support authors you like.

1. Buy their book.
2. Buy a copy as a gift.
3. Read their books where others can see you do so.
4. Ask bookstore employees where his or her books are located, even if you know it's not carried there (it creates demand).
5. Leave a review at Amazon, BN, Goodreads, and elsewhere.
6. Like/Follow the author's social media.
7. Signup for his or mailing list.
8. Follow them on his or her author profile and at Bookbub.
9. Tell someone about a book.
10. Mention/recommend the book on social media.
11. Request the authors' books at your local library.
12. Suggest a book at a local book club.
13. Ask podcasters or other media to interview the author as appropriate.

Get ready for more Faith in Fiction Devotionals…

Faith in Fiction No.2:
Divergents, Tributes, Games, and Sandworms

Coming in 2020!

Made in the USA
Lexington, KY
21 November 2019

57340080R00119